HAPPY ON THE HOMESTRETCH

PAT WILLIAMS
WITH MARK ATTEBERRY

HAPPY ON THE HOMESTRETCH

THIRTY WAYS TO MAKE YOUR LATER YEARS
YOUR GREATER YEARS

 Advantage | Books

Published by Advantage Books, Charleston, South Carolina.
An imprint of Advantage Media.

ADVANTAGE is a registered trademark, and the Advantage colophon is a trademark of Advantage Media Group, Inc.

Printed in the United States of America.

10 9 8 7 6 5 4 3 2 1

ISBN: 978-1-64225-879-0 (Paperback)
ISBN: 978-1-64225-878-3 (eBook)

LCCN: 2023906781

Cover design by David Taylor.
Layout design by Matthew Morse.

This publication is designed to provide accurate and authoritative information in regard to the subject matter covered. It is sold with the understanding that the publisher is not engaged in rendering legal, accounting, or other professional services. If legal advice or other expert assistance is required, the services of a competent professional person should be sought.

Advantage Books is an imprint of Advantage Media Group. Advantage Media helps busy entrepreneurs, CEOs, and leaders write and publish a book to grow their business and become the authority in their field. Advantage authors comprise an exclusive community of industry professionals, idea-makers, and thought leaders. For more information go to **advantagemedia.com**.

To four beloved "Bobbys" from Major League Baseball:

Bobby Shantz, age 97
Bobby Morgan, age 96
Bobby Malkmus, age 91
Bobby Richardson, age 87

CONTENTS

ACKNOWLEDGMENTS

Working with Advantage Media Group is always a pleasure. I want to thank Adam Witty for believing in this book, and his great support team—Laura Rashley, Jacob Hollifield, and David Taylor for shepherding it through the publishing process. I also want to thank my longtime friend and wordsmith, Mark Atteberry, for another fun collaboration.

GIVING "FATHER TIME" A HARD TIME

You can't stop Father Time … but you can slow him down.

—KARL MALONE, NBA HALL OF FAMER

This book on aging has been in the works for about thirty years. I'm eighty-two now as I sit down to work on it, but I was in my fifties when I started preparing. I was in great health and extremely active at the time but under no illusions. I knew I would soon be entering the homestretch of my life. I knew aches and pains were in my future. I knew my stamina would start to diminish little by little at some point. I knew young up-and-comers in the corporate world would come along and try to blow right past me. I knew I would eventually start having senior moments. And yes, I knew there was nothing I could do to stop any of it from happening. As the old saying goes, "Father Time is undefeated."

But it's never been my nature to surrender without a fight. When I have been challenged, I have always stiffened my spine, set my jaw, and said, "Bring it on!" I am happy to report that, for many years now, I have been giving Father Time a hard time. He may eventually beat me, but he'll know he's been in a fight. In case you're wondering what I mean by that, consider the following:

Between the ages of fifty-five and seventy, I competed in fifty-eight marathons, including the Boston Marathon thirteen times. These were not half-marathons; they were full marathons. No, the elite marathoners never felt threatened. In fact, I'm sure they were showered and on their way home before I finished. But finish I did. When people asked me why I was running three or four marathons a year when most people were piled up in their recliners, I told them I was getting in shape for my old age.

I retired from the Orlando Magic at the age of seventy-nine. One month later, I launched what I consider to be the biggest challenge of my professional career: leading the effort to bring Major League Baseball to Orlando. I'm still working on it and have high hopes.

Currently, at the age of eighty-two, I am the host of three separate radio programs. One about sports, another about the Christian life, and a third about politics and history.

I am also serving on the board of directors of a very fine publishing house in South Carolina called Advantage Media.

And finally, I am the curator of the Pat Williams Leadership Library, which is housed in the beautiful First Baptist Church of Orlando. The library is open to the public and consists of my own book collection, about thirty thousand volumes in all, which I am continually adding to.

I should probably also mention that in the middle of all this, I found the time to do a yearslong battle with a terrible cancer called multiple myeloma—and beat it. I was seventy when Dr. Robert Reynolds gave me the diagnosis. The first words out of my mouth were "How long am I going to live, Doc?" He said, "Well, the average is two to three years." That was thirteen years ago and counting.

I don't tell you these things to brag. I know it's only by the grace of Almighty God that I am still kicking. He's been better to me than I ever deserved, and I am deeply grateful. But in conjunction with his grace, I have tried to do my part, and that's what this book is about. There are thirty chapters here, and each one is a tip on how you can make your later years your greater years.

Let me explain that.

When I suggest that your later years can be your "greater" years, I am not trying to con you into believing that somehow, at the age of seventy-five, you're going to be stronger, more athletic, more attractive, or have more endurance than when you were thirty-five. Only a fool would believe such a thing. However, I *am* trying to sell you on the idea that you can be happy on the homestretch. Your life can be richer, of better quality, and more meaningful when you are seventy-five than when you were thirty-five. Yes, I acknowledge that, in a fallen world, anything can happen to derail our best-laid plans. But all things being equal, the suggestions I offer in this book will give you a far greater life than most people experience as their time on earth winds down—and possibly a far greater life than you experienced when you were young.

When the actress Cameron Diaz turned forty, journalists started asking her if she was afraid her career might come to an end because she didn't look twenty-five anymore. I love the answer she gave:

I don't know what life will hold for me. But I am ready. Because I know myself better than I did years ago, and I trust myself to make good decisions, or at least to do my best. Because I value the lessons that I've learned, especially in the last decade, and I look forward to seeing what kinds of new understandings the decades ahead will bring.[1]

We're all like Ms. Diaz in that we don't know what life will hold for us, but we can be ready. That is the purpose of this book. There's no magic here, no hocus-pocus that guarantees a long and prosperous life. But in the pages ahead, I will offer you plenty of ideas on how you can be happy on the homestretch. Or, to put it another way, plenty of ideas on how you can give old Father Time a hard time.

---

1   Cameron Diaz, *The Longevity Book* (New York: HarperCollins, 2016), 12.

CHAPTER 1

RESOLVE YOUR STORY LINES

You can't go back and change the beginning, but you can start where you are and change the ending.

—C. S. LEWIS, AUTHOR

There's long been a debate about which stage of a person's life is most important. I'm sure you've heard it said that a person learns more in the first five years of life than in all the rest of his life put together. I have no trouble believing it. Moving from a completely helpless little bundle to a person who can walk and talk and feed and dress himself is quite a jump.

But some would say the adolescent and young adult years are the most critical. That's the period where you pick a career that's likely going to be your life's work. It's when your work ethic will be established and when your thinking on a host of critical issues will be shaped. It's when you choose a spouse and become a parent. It's hard to overestimate the importance of such choices.

But as important as these stages of life are, I'm convinced that the most important stage is the last one. I'm not sure how our later years came to be called our "golden" years, but in terms of their importance, they really are. The reason is because your later years are that period of your life when all of your story lines will come together and be resolved one way or another.

When you're young, you can (and most people do) wander hither and yon, trying this and that, experiencing good times and bad times. But there's always the knowledge in the back of your mind that you can change course or back up or simply just quit and try something different if things aren't working out. That's not the case when you get older. You know that you're running out of time, that things are winding down, that you're making your final choices, the ones that will determine your legacy.

> *Every* ending is a big ending, especially the ending of a life, because once it ends, there are no more chances to make right anything that has gone wrong.

Have you ever been to a Broadway show? They all open with a big production number, singing and dancing and probably a song that has become famous. Then there's the middle part of the show where the story line takes shape, the tension is created, and the audience is sucked in. But it's the ending that ties it all together. If the show stopped without resolving the plotlines, the audience would revolt. Show people talk about "the big ending." I'm here to tell you that *every* ending is a big ending, especially the ending of a life, because once it ends, there are no more chances to make right anything that has gone wrong.

Allow me to suggest three story lines of your life that will be resolved sooner rather than later and that you should be thinking about.

Story line #1: Your family

I can remember a time when there were still families around that had a kind of *Leave It to Beaver* wholesomeness—no wayward members, no dysfunctional relationships, and no skeletons in the closet. But today such families are extremely rare. The brokenness of our world has become so extreme, so pervasive that virtually no family gets by unscathed.

Is there a dark story line in your family that you could help resolve in a positive way? Is there a prodigal son who needs to come home? Is there an outcast who needs to know he is welcome to come home? Is there a feud that has been boiling far too long? Is there an unresolved issue that makes everyone uncomfortable at family get-togethers? If so, what could you do to help? Maybe stubborn personalities are involved, and no one is willing to make the first move. Why don't you?

Even if your effort bears no fruit, two good things will result: One, you will have the peace of mind that comes from knowing you tried. And two, you will have planted a seed that may bear fruit later. The people involved will remember what you said, and sometime in the future, when they are in a more receptive frame of mind, your words might sink in and bring positive change.

Story line #2: Your reputation

"She's the biggest gossip in town."

"You can't believe a word he says."

"She'll say anything to get what she wants."

"I wouldn't trust him as far as I can throw him."

We've all heard these statements. We've all *made* these statements because we all know people for whom these statements are true. They've spent their lives saying and doing things that cause us not to respect or trust them.

Are you one of those people?

Don't be too quick to say no.

If you have a habit or quality that has diminished you in the eyes of others, it's likely that you've lived with it for so long (or gotten away with it for so long) that you've become blind to it. Also, you shouldn't take comfort in the fact that no one is calling you out. The people who suffer from your character flaws have probably accepted you (or maybe learned to tolerate you), but that doesn't mean they respect you.

Let your later years be years of self-improvement. If you have a reputation for being undependable, start being someone people can count on. If you have a reputation for being cagey, start being honest and open. If you have a reputation for being a blabbermouth, learn to keep your mouth shut. Believe me, people will notice your positive changes. And they *will* think better of you.

Storyline #3: Your attitude

Do you remember the 1993 movie *Grumpy Old Men* with Walter Matthau and Jack Lemmon? It was about two old curmudgeonly guys who constantly insulted and played cruel practical jokes on each other. The comedy was a surprise hit. So much so that the cast reunited for a sequel, *Grumpier Old Men*.

Let me just be clear about one thing: Only in a Hollywood movie is an old curmudgeon funny, let alone two old curmudgeons. In the real world, few things are more unpleasant than a grumpy old person.

Are you a grumpy old person?

I've noticed that a lot of people grow grumpier as they age. When the aches and pains kick in, when technology passes them by and leaves them totally confused, when the kids and grandkids don't stop by as often, and when all of the arts (TV, movies, music, and books) seem to be geared for young people, it's easy to feel bitter. And once bitterness starts creeping in, grumpiness is never far behind.

10

But you have a choice.

You can die with people thinking of you as just a grumpy old man (or woman), or you can rewrite that story line and close out the last act of your life putting smiles on people's faces instead of frowns. You really don't have to complain about every ache and pain. You don't have to point out everything you don't like about the younger generation. You don't have to call every song that comes on the car radio or every new television program trash. Granted, they might be, but you don't have to dwell on it and say it constantly. People don't want to hear it.

Instead, you could focus on things that are positive and good. You could speak well of nice things and nice people. You could smile instead of scowling all the time. You could let yourself laugh when something is funny. One of my favorite quotes is from Henry Ward Beecher. He said, "A person without a sense of humor is like a wagon without springs, jolted by every pebble in the road."

And this is important: You could adopt an attitude toward the things you don't like that says, "These things are not my problem. I can choose not to watch or listen or participate. I'm not going to dwell on them and let them ruin my attitude."

Your family.

Your reputation.

Your attitude.

These are story lines in every person's life. They may take various twists and turns throughout the journey of our lives, but at the end they will be resolved. Everybody loves a happy ending. As long as you're still kicking, you have a chance to write one.

CHAPTER 2

WAVE BYE-BYE

Time may be a great healer, but it's a lousy beautician.

—DOROTHY PARKER, WRITER

Aging is very much about goodbyes.

When you're born, you say goodbye to the womb.

Sometime later you say goodbye to diapers and the bottle.

At some time during childhood, you say goodbye to dolls or toy trucks.

When you start dating someone special, you say goodbye to playing the field.

When you get married, you say goodbye to living only for yourself.

When you become a parent, you say goodbye to sleep.

Then when you reach your later years, rather than tapering off, the goodbyes start coming fast and furious. You say goodbye to your hair, your energy, your stamina, your memory, your flexibility, your reflexes, your eyesight, your hearing, and sadly, a lot of your friends.

Goodbyes are traditionally thought of as sad or tragic. For example, Hollywood knows that one plot device they can always count on to get an emotional reaction from the audience is the sad goodbye. Remember when Dorothy said goodbye to the Scarecrow, the Tin Man, and the Cowardly Lion before returning to Kansas? Or more recently, maybe you remember Frodo's heartbreaking goodbye to his best friend, Sam, at the end of the *Lord of the Rings* trilogy. Such scenes are rendered with soaring orchestral music that is guaranteed to put a tear on the cheek of even the most stonehearted person.

But I want to challenge you to rethink some of the goodbyes we are forced to say as we age. They are not all so terrible. Consider the following simple truths.

First, many of the things we say goodbye to, we can live without and still be perfectly happy. Take hair, for example. Lots of guys fear hair loss as if it were a direct threat to their manhood. YouGov reports that 59 percent of men between the ages of eighteen and twenty-four are "terrified" by the prospect of losing their hair. Interestingly, the same survey reports that only 14 percent of men age sixty-five and older care about losing their hair.[2] You know why older guys don't care as much? Because they've started losing (or have already lost) their hair and realize that it's not nearly as big a deal as they thought it would be. You can live a perfectly happy and fulfilling life with a lot of hair, a little hair, or no hair.

And by the way, never overlook the fact that numerous bald men have won the title of "World's Sexiest Man," including Prince William, Vin Diesel, and Dwayne "the Rock" Johnson. These winners mesh

---

2   Linley Sanders, "Most young people are 'terrified' of going bald," November 2020, accessed February 17, 2023, YouGovAmerica, https://today.yougov.com/topics/health/articles-reports/2020/11/10/terrified-going-bald-poll.

with a survey done by Skull Shaver, which revealed that 87.5 percent of women of different ages and nationalities find bald men attractive.[3]

Another thing you can live without is the stamina of youth. People in their twenties can play thirty-six holes of golf in a day with no problem. People in their forties and fifties usually stick to eighteen. People in their seventies or eighties often just play nine. The point is, they're all enjoying golf at whatever level is comfortable for them.

So many things in life work this way. Like gardening, for example. If you enjoy planting and cultivating a garden, you can still do it even if your stamina isn't what it used to be. Just do it in a few shorter shifts instead of one long one. In pretty much all of life, the key is adjustments. You can enjoy all of the pleasures of youth as you age if you're willing to adjust.

Second, saying goodbye to some things of value actually makes us better people. I mentioned earlier in this book that I ran fifty-eight marathons between the ages of fifty-five and seventy. Then at seventy, cancer struck, and I had to wave bye-bye to my passion for running. Nobody runs marathons with multiple myeloma. But going through that experience gave me a level of empathy for other cancer patients that I had never had before. I suddenly understood the challenge and struggle on an emotional level rather than just an intellectual level, which made me a better person. I even wrote a book called *The Mission Is Remission: Hope for Battling Cancer*, something I would not have done otherwise. Even today I have a level of compassion for people with serious illnesses that far exceeds what I had before. When the opportunity arises, I talk to people and try to encourage them, and I'm convinced that I'm more effective because I've walked the road myself.

---

3   Edita Revazyan, "Do Women Find Bald Men Attractive?," Skull Shaver, October 2022, accessed February 17, 2023, https://skullshaver.eu/blogs/news/do-women-find-bald-men-attractive.

Saying goodbye to things we cherish can also make us more grateful for the things that remain. Take a wife whose husband passes away. She will be heartbroken, of course. But the experience could well cause her to cherish her friends and neighbors more and build deeper relationships with them. Or she might draw closer to her children and grandchildren.

And yet another way we can become better people is by replacing the things we say goodbye to with new things that are more significant or important. One person was phased out of his job because of downsizing and found it difficult to find new employment because of his age. So he took retirement and started volunteering for a nonprofit. It was while working for that nonprofit that he found an undiscovered passion and what he called his "true purpose." But he might never have found it if he hadn't had to wave bye-bye to his career.

Third, saying goodbye to things as we grow older is God's way of preparing us to say goodbye to this world. Most young people rarely think about death, and when they do, they see it as something big and dark and scary. They hear an elderly person talk about being ready to die, and they can't relate to it. It makes no sense to them. They can't imagine feeling that way.

Well, of course, they can't!

When you're young and healthy and full of hopes and dreams and plans for the future, not to mention in love or married or with children of your own, death isn't even a tiny blip on your radar. Your life trajectory is up, up, up! But little by little, as we age, the hopes and dreams are fulfilled (or adjusted to be more realistic and *then* fulfilled), the story of the marriage is written, the kids are raised, and suddenly, a sense of fulfillment starts to take over. The trajectory levels off. We start slowing down and, yes, thinking about death more. And for the first time, it doesn't seem so big and dark and scary. Especially for people of faith who believe in heaven.

But the things we say goodbye to are an important piece of the process. Whether it's your hair or your energy or your eyesight, you learn the fine art of letting go, which ulti- mately makes it easier to let go of this world.

As you age, don't see those waving bye-bye moments as sad. See them as a continuing part of the process of living. Remember, you've been saying goodbye to things since the day you were born. It's really nothing new.

> As you age, don't see those waving bye-bye moments as sad. See them as a continu- ing part of the process of living.

CHAPTER 3

BE PATIENT WITH YOUNGER PEOPLE

*I was so naive as a kid I used to sneak
behind the barn and do nothing.*

—JOHNNY CARSON, TV HOST

Young people are often annoyed by older people. One reason is because we move slower, and young people always seem to be in a hurry. You know you're getting older when younger people routinely zip around you and fly past you in supermarkets and shopping malls and theme parks.

We also drive slower. Jerry Seinfeld did an entire routine on the driving habits of senior citizens. He said, "They drive slow and sit low. The state flag of Florida should be a steering wheel with a hat and two knuckles on it." And of course, he made a joke about how we have been known to drive for miles with our turn signals on. He said that many older people turn it on in the morning and let it run all day.

Okay, so maybe we are a bit annoying to younger people. But they are annoying to us too. One reason is because of their cluelessness. They just don't seem to know things that they *should* know— things that we knew when we were their age.

For example, George Burns, who made countless jokes about his age, once did a show on a college campus. After the performance, several students came backstage to talk to him. One student asked him if he really did get his start as a dancer. George said that he did and then made a joke about how he once asked Betsy Ross to dance, but she turned him down because she was too busy sewing something.

The students didn't get the joke. They just stared at him. Most people would have laughed because of the suggestion that George was around in the 1700s and also because he was too dumb to know what Betsy was sewing. Finally, one of the students asked if Betsy Ross was a good dancer. Another asked why she didn't take a break from sewing for a few minutes and dance with him. A third one said, "Is Betsy Ross Diana Ross's sister?" And yet another said, "Who's Diana Ross?"

It would be interesting to know who gives the most eye rolls: young people because of old people or old people because of young people.

I've done my share of eye-rolling just this week. I've been watching my favorite baseball team, the Philadelphia Phillies, play in the World Series. One young Phillies outfielder has the kind of hair and beard you would expect to see on a caveman. In fact, I suspect that even a caveman would tell him he needed a haircut. I'm sure he's a nice young man, but every time I see him, I feel like launching a conspiracy to have him kidnapped and dragged to a barbershop.

But even as I confess my frustration to you, I challenge you to do what I try to do: keep a lid on it. Be patient with younger people, even if they aren't always patient with you. There are three reasons why this is a good idea.

A first reason why it's good to be patient with young people is because it's a pointless waste of emotional energy to worry about things you have no control over. Every now and then, I will see a street preacher in Orlando, some guy standing on a street corner with a little amplifier and a microphone. He will also have a homemade sign warning of impending doom unless people repent. Even on the hottest, most humid summer days, he will be standing in the blazing Florida sun, waving his Bible, and screaming at the passing traffic. Of course, no one—and I do mean *no one*—is paying any attention to him. The people passing by on foot give him a wide berth, and the people in cars have their windows rolled up and don't hear a word he's saying.

Old people who fret and stew and whine and complain about younger people are very much like that street preacher. They may be spewing out the words, but no one is paying any attention. There's not a chance—none whatsoever—that your complaining about younger people is going to change them. So what's the point of carrying on? If you have some energy, why not invest it in a pursuit that stands a chance of bearing some kind of fruit?

A second reason why it's good to be patient with younger people is because they can be a blessing to you, and you to them, if you don't alienate them first. I know what you're thinking: "What? Me be blessed by some young person who's all tatted up and has a ring in his nose and looks like he hasn't cut or combed his hair in a month?" Yes, that's exactly what I'm suggesting could happen.

Nowadays, there are two groups of people that are suffering a loneliness epidemic. Those two groups are seniors and school-age kids. Seniors because they see a big drop in their social lives when they retire and leave the workplace and because they often outlive their spouses

21

and friends. Simultaneously, many school kids suffer from loneliness because they come from broken families or because their parents work long hours and are rarely home. Capitalizing on this great intergenerational need, many organizations are springing up that are determined to build a bridge between the two groups. They recognize that older people have many years of experience and time to spare, while younger people need guidance and encouragement and often have skills they can share that older people need. Bringing the two groups together only makes sense.

> You and that strange-looking young person could actually become allies and, yes, friends if you can keep an open mind and refrain from being judgmental.

One simple example of a highly successful intergenerational program is where seniors can sign up to have a young person tutor them on the use of technology. What senior doesn't need a little help with their computer or cell phone? And at the same time, the young person has a purpose, gains the satisfaction that comes from helping someone, and possibly makes a new friend.

My point is that you and that strange-looking young person could actually become allies and, yes, friends if you can keep an open mind and refrain from being judgmental. Young and old go together a lot better than most people think, which reminds me of a great story.

A young boy was outside a bar fishing in a small water hole that obviously didn't have any fish in it. It really wasn't much more than a large puddle, but he was sitting there on an overturned bucket with his line in the water. A man coming out of the bar saw the boy and walked over. He asked the boy his name, and the two of them struck up a conversation. Before long, the man was sitting on the grass beside the boy, shooting the breeze. Finally, the man decided to play along with the boy's little game. He said, "You catching anything?" The boy said, "You're the fourth one today."

And a third reason why it's good to be patient with young people is because there was a time when you annoyed older people too. It's one of the unchangeable facts of life, as dependable as gravity or the sun coming up in the east every morning: young people seem crazy to older people. Do you think that fact was suddenly suspended when you were a teenager and then reinstated when you became an adult? No, it wasn't. However sane and normal and well-adjusted you think you were as a young person, I promise there were older people who looked at you and just shook their heads. They looked at me that way too. The least we can do is not take the same attitude toward young people that we hated when older people took it toward us.

CHAPTER 4

THROW AWAY THE TOUPEE

Nothing makes a woman look so old as
desperately trying to look young.

—COCO CHANEL, FASHION DESIGNER

You've seen them, and they make you cringe.

The older man wearing a bad toupee. His eyebrows and whiskers are gray, but the rug on his head is jet-black. Even worse, you've seen that hairstyle before, back in the 1960s, when the Beatles arrived in America.

The older man with a severe comb-over. Hair that sprouted out of his scalp just above one ear is laid up and over the top of his head, stopping just above the other ear. You can't help wondering what it must feel like when the hair on one side of your head is an inch long, and on the other side, it's a foot long.

The older woman wearing short shorts and a skimpy top. You figure she might have looked pretty good in that outfit forty years ago. Or forty pounds ago. She seems like a nice person, and you're sure she has many friends, but you know spandex is not one of them.

The older woman who's obviously had some "work" done. You take one look at her and remember the old Joan Rivers line: "I've had so much plastic surgery, when I die they will donate my body to Tupperware."

Almost everywhere you go, you will encounter older people trying desperately to look younger. I imagine our Founding Fathers would find this quite shocking since they were obsessed with looking older and wiser. Remember those white wigs they wore? Yes, that was the point of those funny-looking things. Today everything has changed. Hair dyes, hair regrowth products, Botox, Viagra, wrinkle-removing creams, and a whole range of cosmetic surgeries make it possible for older people to try to hang on to their youth or at least the image of youth.

It is certainly not my place to criticize anyone for choosing one of these products or procedures. People are free to make their own decisions. But I would like to offer a few truths for those on the homestretch of life to think about.

First, the appearance of youth is not youth. At sixty-five, you might have a facelift that makes you look fifty-five. But you did not turn back the clock. You're still sixty-five. Looking fifty in the face doesn't make your arthritis disappear. It doesn't mean your troublesome gallbladder is going to suddenly stop bothering you. It doesn't make you tech-savvy if you weren't before. And it certainly doesn't prevent you from having "senior moments."

We live in a generation that speaks of "identifying" as this or that. A man says he identifies as a woman, or a woman identifies as a man. But intellectually honest people know that "identifying" is not actually "being," no matter how much we might want it to be. Likewise, an older person might "identify" as a younger person by having cosmetic surgery or dressing young or grooving to the latest popular songs. But sixty-five is still sixty-five, even if you do have fewer wrinkles, thanks to the surgeon's scalpel.

Second, chasing the "image" of youth doesn't fool anybody. Or maybe I should put it this way: when you chase the image of youth—when you do everything in your power to look younger—the only people you fool are total strangers who don't know you. For example, when you have a facelift, strangers might look at you and think you look ten years younger than you really are. But the people who knew you before the facelift will think, "She looks good. But she *should* look good after spending all that money on a facelift." Maybe it's just me, but it seems like that would take a lot of the satisfaction out of looking younger. Is it really worth all that money and pain to fool only those people who don't know you?

Third, in a generation of artificial everything, authenticity is more refreshing than ever. Do you remember the first time you were in a restaurant or supermarket and realized that they're now making meat out of plants? Or I should say, they're making plants look like meat. Brands like Beyond Meat or Impossible or Tofurky look like meat but aren't. Or how about the movies? Most of the action you see in big-budget movies is computer generated. And those celebrity movie stars are definitely *not* doing those dangerous stunts, though it looks like they are. And then there's virtual reality. By definition it is "an artificial environment which is experienced through sensory stimuli (such as sights and sounds) provided by a computer and in which one's actions partially determine what happens in the environment."[4] Don't you sometimes get the feeling that almost nothing is real anymore?

This is one big reason why I find authenticity so refreshing. Things that are real may not be as slick and perfect on the surface; they

---

4   Merriam-Webster, Definition: Virtual Reality, accessed February 17, 2023, https://www.merriam-webster.com/dictionary/virtual%20reality.

may not be as pretty to the eye, but they seem somehow more precious because they are genuine. When I see elderly people who are wrinkled and stooped, I can't help wondering what amazing things they have done, what interesting places they have been, and what fascinating stories they could tell. In fact, I've spoken at length with many elderly people, such as John Wooden, as I have gathered material for the books I have written. In every case, they made no attempt to seem like anything but who they were. They acknowledged and embraced their age and their aches and pains and struggles. Trying to project some false image never entered their minds.

Jamie Lee Curtis is an actress who has a lot to say about aging. She admits to having had cosmetic surgery, but she says it was a mistake. Not because it didn't make some wrinkles go away but because it made her seem not as real. "I put Botox in my head. Does Botox make the big wrinkle go away? Yes. But then you look like a plastic figurine," she said.[5] Ms. Curtis now calls herself "pro-aging." In other words, she's for going through the aging process without a fight, embracing whatever it brings, and being real to the very end.

My recommendation to you is to do the same. I'm not standing in judgment of you if you've had a procedure or maybe bought an outfit that's a little young for your demographic. And certainly, if you need a knee replacement or a hip replacement to be able to remain mobile, you should take advantage of whatever medical technology offers to maintain a great quality of life. But will fewer wrinkles really improve your quality of life? Will a bad toupee make you more attractive to women? Will pouring yourself into a pair of spandex short

---

5   Marianne Garvey, "Jamie Lee Curtis has aging advice: 'Don't mess with your face," CNN, October 2022, February 17, 2023, https://www.cnn.com/2022/10/12/ entertainment/jamie-lee-curtis-age-aging-advice-face.

shorts and a halter top make you *not* look sixty? These questions all have the same answer: no.

The one thing that will always look good on you is authenticity. Another is good character. I long for a time when the mileage that shows on people's bodies is seen as a badge of honor—a tribute to grit and survival—and good character is seen as being far more valuable than the ability to fool people who don't know you into thinking you're a few years younger than you really are.

> The one thing that will always look good on you is authenticity. Another is good character.

CHAPTER 5

BREAK UP WITH THE GOOD OLD DAYS

Holding on is believing that there's only a past;
letting go is knowing that there's a future.

—DAPHNE ROSE KINGMA, AUTHOR

There is a tendency in aging people to cling to the "good old days."

It happens in church: "I miss the good old days when we used to sing hymns. I just don't like these new songs, and the band is way too loud!"

It happens with pop culture: "I miss the good old days when every other word on TV and in the movies wasn't a curse word."

It happens with technology: "I miss the good old days when a phone was just a phone, and you didn't have to have a degree in computer science to use it."

It happens with the media: "I miss the good old days with guys like Tom Brokaw or Walter Cronkite. Today the news is just a bunch of people yelling and arguing all the time."

Be honest. Are you in love with the good old days? Do you often find yourself pining for a time when things were much simpler, much slower-paced, much less stressful, much *more* to your liking? Do you find yourself often bringing up the past in conversations? Do you resist new ideas by always talking about how great things used to be and how more change just takes us away from what was once ideal? Do you secretly take pleasure when new, innovative ideas don't fly and the status quo has to be resumed? Do you stubbornly refuse to embrace new technologies, such as online banking or online giving to your church? And do you take pride in being a holdout?

Let me be quick to say that I know these feelings well. At my age, and with the world changing so rapidly, I would *love* to go back in time. I still remember the day my family ganged up on me and made me get a new cell phone. It might as well have been a spaceship. I looked at that thing and thought, "You and me are not going to get along!" And we don't. I always feel like it is secretly plotting my demise. I would rather use my trusty Franklin Planner than the contacts in my phone. It has been a faithful friend for many, many years and never once malfunctioned. And I don't have to remember to plug it in!

But let's be honest.

The good old days were not as good as we make them out to be.

Before you throw this book across the room, hear me out.

Back in 1977, John Claypool wrote a book titled *Stages*. In that book he examined the predictable crises people face in different stages of life. I was taken by this passage, which was written by a woman he knew:

I loved my uncle's ranch when I was a child. There was space to run unhampered, freedom to explore. The dust lay inches thick on the trails, and running barefoot down the path of sifting powder was a sumptuous sort of feeling. The barn was my playground, full of animated toys. In the loft there were hay and mice and fairly friendly spiders. The mint grew wild and plush beside the creek, and my aunt made berry pies and the smell would seek me out whenever I played around the house. I rode my cousin's palomino through fantasies that never seemed to end.

But if I am not careful, Lord, I can edit these memories and forget that I got a bee sting where I picked the mint and burned my tongue time and time again on the berry pies because I never seemed to learn and couldn't wait. Or that the barn smelled just awful or that the horse made my bottom sore and the dust that felt like sifted powder made me sneeze all summer. If I'm not careful, I can forget all these things. But if I am wise, I will remember that all of life has both of these things in it.[6]

You might wonder what makes us only remember the good stuff and forget the things that weren't so wonderful. I'm not an expert, but it seems to me that our minds work like a record store. Today's record stores sell the good and the bad of today's music. But of yesterday's music, they sell only the good stuff, the hits, the classics everybody loves. Likewise, it's as if our brains naturally let go of unpleasantness and only remember the good stuff. As a baseball player, for example, I can easily remember the clutch hits I got. I can even remember the pitcher's name and the count and how many runners were on base. But I'm a little fuzzy on all those strikeouts.

Here are a couple of suggestions.

First, don't be so obsessed with the good old days that you fail to appreciate the good things that are happening today. It's great to have fond memories, but never forget that today things are happening that will become fond memories for today's young people. Wouldn't it be nice if you could notice and enjoy those things too? Technology is a

---

6   John Claypool, *Stages* (Waco: Word, Incorporated, 1980), 86.

good example. Yes, it's frustrating and confusing. There is a tendency for us older folks to throw our hands up and say, "No more!" But it's that technology that allows you to stay in better touch with your loved ones through Skype or Zoom or FaceTime. It's that technology that allows you to have things you enjoy at your fingertips. Things like newspapers and music and movies and television shows—even television shows that you love from years gone by! It's that technology that allows you to send free emails instantly instead of constantly buying stamps to put on letters that will take days to reach their destination. Only the crustiest of curmudgeons will fail to see what wonderful things we have to enjoy today.

> Don't be so obsessed with the good old days that you fail to appreciate the good things that are happening today.

Second, keep in mind that an obsession with the past can be discouraging to people who are trying hard to make things better today. Churches, for example, are always trying to grow, which means they're implementing new ideas and programs to try to reach more people. Imagine how discouraging it is to your pastor when you greet every new idea with a roll of the eyes and shake of the head and a snide comment about how the church just isn't what it used to be. The same thing can happen in the workplace. Your company decides to introduce policies and procedures that it believes will streamline the business and make it healthier, but it's different from what has become comfortable for you, so you gripe and complain and poison the atmosphere in the office. Don't be that person who is seen as an obstacle or, worse yet, a cancer to the culture of the team.

To use dating as a metaphor, I would recommend that you break up with the good old days and just become good friends. Enjoy your fond memories, yes. But don't let them deceive you into believing that today isn't wonderful as well. Every generation offers plenty to enjoy and be thankful for.

CHAPTER 6

LET TOMORROW TAKE CARE OF ITSELF

*Live every day as if it were your last because
someday you're going to be right.*

—MUHAMMAD ALI, HEAVYWEIGHT BOXING CHAMPION

Tomorrow is one of the great obsessions of the human race. Virtually everything we have done—invented, built, or explored—has been with an eye toward tomorrow, to make things better. Even the choices we make on a daily basis:

Exercising.

Eating healthy.

Going to college.

Getting married.

Having children.

Disciplining those children.

Buying food at the supermarket.

Changing the oil in the car.

Going to the doctor for a checkup.

Buying insurance.

Making a will.

We do it all with one eye on tomorrow. We know we can't guarantee a bright tomorrow because life is just too unpredictable. But we know that if we don't make smart choices, we will have no tomorrow worth living.

I've noticed that when we are young, our thoughts of tomorrow center around big life choices: who to marry, what career to pursue, where to live. But as we move into middle age, our thoughts of tomorrow begin to narrow. Many of the big life issues that occupied our minds when we were young have long been settled, so we think about smaller things, such as how much exercise we should get, what vitamins and supplements we should take, what foods give us indigestion, and so on.

But then we come to yet another stage of life: the homestretch. On the homestretch of life, some very unsettling questions start to creep into our minds:

My eyes and reflexes aren't very good. What happens if I can't drive anymore?

My legs are getting weak. What if I can't get up and down the steps of my house?

My medications are so expensive. What if I can't afford them anymore?

I've heard horror stories about nursing homes. What if I have to go live in one?

These are not just questions. They're fears. They're worries. And they can make it very hard for people to be happy on the homestretch.

Research shows that anxiety is a common problem among older people and that those who suffer from it rarely get help. Sometimes they convince themselves that they're okay when they're really not. (All ages of people do this!) Sometimes they shame themselves for their feelings: "I should be thankful. I'm in much better shape than most of my friends." And sometimes they keep things bottled up because they don't want to be a problem or a burden to their loved ones. Unfortunately, ignoring our worries and fears only allows them to grow.

I am not a doctor or psychologist, but I have a few suggestions if you're struggling with anxiety on the homestretch of your life.

First, talk to your doctor. Isn't this what you would do if you had a shooting pain down your leg or an ache in your abdomen? Sure you would. But for some reason, when it comes to mental/emotional aches and pains, we think we should be able to manage them on our own. Never forget that physical ailments (diabetes, for example) can cause mood swings and depression. At the very least, your doctor will be able to see if there's anything going on in your body that you're not aware of and treat it if there is.

Second, make sure you have some positive people in your life. Older people can fall into the trap of hanging out with other older people and spending all their time talking about their aches and pains and problems. It's called a pity party. Whatever you do, don't let your life become one big pity party.

I would suggest that you find things to do that are inherently positive and upbeat. Does your church have a senior's ministry? Seniors groups are notorious for having fun and eating large amounts of food. Get involved! Or maybe you could ask a couple of your more positive friends to have a weekly lunch date. Be adventurous and try some new restaurants. Or perhaps you could do some volunteer work at the hospital. Helping to bring a little joy into the lives of people who are going through a hard time is a surefire way to make yourself feel better.

Third, simply to let tomorrow take care of itself. Jesus said, "Don't worry about tomorrow. It will take care of itself" (Matt. 6:34, CEV). That is some of the greatest advice ever given and especially applicable to older people. Life unfolds a day at a time. Each day brings a new set of circumstances, and we deal with them then. It's called "crossing the bridge when you come to it."

> Life unfolds a day at a time. Each day brings a new set of circumstances, and we deal with them then.

One woman was having trouble getting up the steps to her porch. One weekend she went to visit her daughter and grandkids. When she returned, she had a beautiful new ramp that allowed her to walk up onto her porch with ease. It turned out that her daughter made all the arrangements for the ramp to be built while she was gone. It completely solved her problem and was a beautiful expression of love from her daughter. The point is, when the problem arose, it was solved. The bridge was crossed when she came to it.

This is how life works but especially on the homestretch. In fact, some have described aging as the navigation of challenges. When we are young and hurdles appear in front of us, we just leap over them and go on our way. When we get older, it takes more thought, and sometimes we go around instead of over. But we still navigate them! You will navigate your challenges too. Tomorrow will take care of itself.

Let me offer one more thought in closing.

Many of the bridges we think are out there in front of us never materialize. Just because you have family members who lived out their lives in a nursing home doesn't mean you will end up in one. Just because you know older people who fell and broke a hip doesn't mean you will. Just because not driving anymore seems like it will be the end of the world for you doesn't mean it will. It just might remove a lot of stress from your life.

When Jesus said that tomorrow will take care of itself, I think at least part of what he meant was that tomorrow might not even look like you think it's going to look. Why do we assume that tomorrow is always going to be bad? Tomorrow is notoriously full of surprises. It might turn out to be a whole lot better than you think. But even if it isn't, it will take care of itself whether you worry about it or not. So why worry?

CHAPTER 7

LIVE ABOVE THE STEREOTYPE

*Hopefully I'm not a grumpy old guy sitting in
the corner, yelling at people and demanding things.*

—GEORGE W. BUSH, FORMER PRESIDENT OF THE UNITED STATES

It's interesting that as you age, you begin to notice things that swept right past you when you were young. For example, I've been noticing how television commercials stereotype older people. Perhaps you've seen the one that shows a gray-haired couple talking to their grandson about his baseball game on a speakerphone. You can see the boy's words being spelled out closed-captioned style on a small screen. The couple is not incapacitated. They look perfectly healthy and normal except, of course, that using a phone is difficult for them. They need closed-captioned and buttons as big as quarters to make a call.

Another commercial for Medicare Advantage insurance plans shows an older woman with a scowling expression saying she's not going to call the number on the screen. The voice-over artist enumerates one reason after another why it's smart to call, but the cranky old woman on the screen continues to stubbornly say she's not going to call, until the very end when she finally relents.

And then, of course, there are the Progressive commercials that show young homeowners turning into their parents. Dr. Rick holds teaching sessions and takes them on outings in the community to try to teach them not to be like their silly, clueless parents.

My challenge to you in this chapter is to live above the stereotype.

What does this mean?

It means you don't settle for what is typically expected of people who are aging.

Take retirement, for example. In most people's minds, retirement is synonymous with quitting work. "Oh, he doesn't work anymore. He's retired." The truth is, according to a Pew Research survey, only 27 percent of retired people say they have *not* worked for pay since they retired.[7] Meaning, of course, that almost three out of four have!

Back in 2019, you may remember that ABC broadcasted live performances of two classic sitcom episodes, one of *All in the Family* and one of *The Jeffersons*. Obviously, the original stars from the 1970s were replaced by younger actors. Woody Harrelson and Marisa Tomei played Archie and Edith Bunker, and George and Louise Jefferson were played by Jamie Foxx and Wanda Sykes. But here's the interesting thing about that broadcast event. Norman Lear, who originated those classic shows, hosted the event with Jimmy Kimmel. Norman was ninety-six at the time. Talk about living above the stereotype! Most ninety-six-year-olds are not hosting groundbreaking television events!

---

7   Pew Research Center Press Release, "Working After Retirement: The Gap Between Expectations and Reality," Pew Research Center, accessed February 17, 2023, https://www.pewresearch.org/wp-content/uploads/sites/3/2010/10/Retirement.pdf.

So am I saying you should still be working at the age of ninety-six? No. Living above the stereotype means four things.

First, living above the stereotype means continuing to live according to your abilities. Some golfers can't wait until they officially become a "senior" so they can move up to the senior tees and gain a great advantage over their younger golfing buddies. That's fine if your age really has robbed you of the ability to play a competitive game, but a "senior" golfer is only fifty years old! Many "seniors" are vibrant and healthy and strong. I say you should keep living (and playing) according to your abilities and not your privileges.

One man I heard about had heart surgery and was given a handicapped parking pass by his doctor. But he never used it. He always parked away from the entrance and walked, for two reasons. One, he felt he needed the exercise. And two, he knew the handicapped spaces were limited and felt there were others who needed them more than he did. That's living above the stereotype.

> Live above the stereotype by keeping your opinions to yourself. Accept what you can't change. Just roll with it and focus on those things you do like.

Second, living above the stereotype means accepting cultural trends. Notice, I didn't say that living above the stereotype means *liking* cultural trends. There will never come a day when I will like seeing young people with pieces of metal sticking out of their noses or with purple hair. But at the same time, I don't have to roll my eyes and shake my head and criticize every time I see such a thing. Far too many older people are too outspoken about their personal dislikes, which is why we get a reputation for being cranky and mean. Live above the stereotype by keeping your opinions to yourself. Accept what you can't change. Just roll with it and focus on those things you do like.

Third, living above the stereotype means keeping your mind active. Perhaps you've noticed that older people talk a lot about the weather, the traffic, their aches and pains, and their doctor appointments. Sometimes I think that if those topics were suddenly off-limits, older people wouldn't have anything to talk about. Why does this happen? I believe it's because people aren't feeding their minds.

If you know anything about me, you know that I am a big proponent of reading. Not trash but books that will help you learn and grow and expand your mind. Throughout my life I have been a reader, and those thousands of books I've read have shaped me, equipped me, and kept me relevant in a fast-moving, ever-changing world. One of the reasons I don't sit around whining about the traffic, the weather, or my aches and pains is because I am still reading and stretching my mind. When I meet a friend for lunch, I have all kinds of things on my mind I want to share and talk about.

If you're not reading, you should be. Or at least listening to audiobooks or podcasts, anything that will stimulate your mind. The great news is that it's not like it used to be when you were in school. There's no one telling you what you *have* to read. You get to pick! And in this generation, there are mountains of choices on every conceivable subject. There's really no excuse for you not to keep your mind active.

And finally, living above the stereotype means continuing to exert influence. In Kissimmee, Florida, an elderly man who had been a minister all his life had to move into a nursing home. He wasn't thrilled about it. Who would be? But he accepted his life circumstances and determined to make the best of it. About a month after he moved in, his much younger preacher stopped in for a visit but couldn't find him. He wasn't in his room, wasn't in the lunchroom, and wasn't outdoors on the patio. The visiting preacher asked an employee where he might be able to find the man. The woman looked at her watch and said, "Oh, he'll be in room 108. He leads a Bible study in that room every day about this time." So the preacher walked to room 108, and sure enough, there was the elderly minister along with several other people in wheelchairs gathered in a circle. He was teaching them the Word of God.

That man was definitely living above the stereotype. He may have been put in a nursing home, but he definitely wasn't put out to pasture. He was still doing what he had always done—helping people draw near to God.

Think about the words that are often used to describe old people.

Curmudgeon.

Old fogy.

Over the hill.

Blue hair.

Old coot.

Geezer.

Codger.

These words reinforce the unbecoming stereotype of older people. The best way to fight against them is to live in such a way that they don't apply. Live above the stereotype.

CHAPTER 8

REMEMBER, OTHER PEOPLE ARE AGING TOO

*There is nothing so moving—not even acts of love or
hate—as the discovery that one is not alone.*

—ROBERT ARDREY, PLAYWRIGHT

In the annals of fictional cowboys, one of the most popular ever created
was the Lone Ranger. His backstory is that he was John Reid, the sole
survivor of a six-man squad of Texas Rangers that was ambushed by
a gang of ruthless outlaws. As he lay wounded and dying, a Native
American named Tonto happened by, found him, and nursed him
back to health. The two men then decided to hunt down the gang that
attacked the rangers and bring them to justice. Reid fashioned a mask
to hide his identity from the gang, and the Lone Ranger was born.

Today we most often refer to the Lone Ranger when talking
about going it alone: "I feel like the Lone Ranger. I have no help" or
"Don't worry, you won't be the Lone Ranger. We'll give you plenty
of help."

One of the very best things about aging is that you aren't the Lone Ranger. As this book is being written, there are fifty-six million people in the United States over the age of sixty-five. By 2030 there will be around seventy million. By 2050 there will be eighty-five million.[8] Right now about one out of every six people you meet on the street is sixty-five or older. No, you are definitely not the Lone Ranger.

Let me offer three reasons why this is good news.

First, the large number of aging people all around you means there are plenty of people around who understand what you're going through. Nothing is harder to deal with than the feeling of being alone. It can hit you when a loved one, especially a spouse, dies. It can hit you when you move someplace where you don't know anyone. It can hit you when you start a new job and feel like everyone in the building knows more than you. And it can hit you when you're going through something and feel like no one around you understands. If you're on the homestretch of life, you've probably had that feeling when it comes to aging. Your stamina, your aches and pains, your cluelessness with technology, your outdated taste in music, and your desire to eat dinner at four o'clock in the afternoon are the source of jokes and gentle prodding by the younger people around you. Naturally, you laugh along to be a good sport (because you know they don't mean any harm), but deep down you feel like they don't understand.

> The large number of aging people all around you means there are plenty of people around who understand what you're going through.

---

8   America's Health Rankings, "Public Health Impact: Population Ages 65+," accessed February 17, 2023, https://www.americashealthrankings.org/explore/senior/measure/pct_65plus/state/ALL.

There's also that moment when the younger people in your family—your kids and grandkids—start making big plans and never stop to think that what is so easy for them feels to you like climbing Mt. Everest. Like going to a theme park, for example. They're all brimming with energy and ready to fly out the door and pile in the car, while you're groaning inwardly at the thought of being on your feet all day.

Well, rejoice! You're not the Lone Ranger! All around you there are people who know exactly how you feel. I highly recommend that you connect with them. You might find a seniors Bible study group through your church. Perhaps you could find a book club through your local library. Maybe there's a local chapter of the Red Hat Society or a SilverSneakers group that meets regularly for exercise. You might be surprised how good it feels to be around people who "get" what you're going through.

Second, the large number of aging people all around you means you have plenty of opportunities to serve others. According to Zippia, there were 25,514 nursing homes in America in 2022. In those homes were 1,246,079 residents.[9] Do you know how many nursing home residents never get a visitor? According to the *Atlanta Journal-Constitution*, it's about 60 percent.[10] Imagine over 600,000 elderly people sitting in America's nursing homes and *never* getting a visitor!

What an opportunity for you, if you are able, to make a difference in someone's life. No doubt there is a nursing home near you. You could go there and talk to the administrator. Ask for the name

9   Abby McCain, "25 Insightful Nursing Home Statistics [2023]: Residents, Locations, and Long-Term Care," Zippia, December 2022, February 17, 2023, https://www.zippia.com/advice/nursing-home-statistics/.

10 Tom Underwood, "Forgotten seniors need time, care," *The Atlanta Journal-Constitution,* October 2010, February 17, 2023, https://www.ajc.com/news/opinion/forgotten-seniors-need-time-care/s6mdH3uUuYzZRcApmVYmvL/.

of a resident who never (or seldom) has a visitor. Then march down the hall, walk into that person's room, and make a new friend. Your friendship and regular visits could be the happiest thing to happen to that person in years.

And remember this: you don't have to do much of anything to make a huge difference in a nursing home resident's life. One man I heard about visited an elderly gentleman once a week. The old man had been an avid reader all his life, but his eyesight had deteriorated to the point that he could no longer see the words. So his visitor brought with him a book of short mystery stories and read them aloud.

Your church probably also has a list of shut-ins who aren't yet ready for a nursing home but also aren't able to drive. What a wonderful thing it would be if you took such a person out to lunch once or twice a month or to the mall to do a little shopping. Yes, they would love the lunch and the shopping, but I promise the best feeling for them would come from just knowing they are not forgotten and that someone cares.

Finally, the large number of aging people around you means that you have a great opportunity to be inspired and encouraged. I've been around athletes all my life. World-class athletes who have astounding ability. And yes, I have marveled at what they can do. But the greatest inspiration I have received has come from older people—people who couldn't dribble a basketball the length of the floor or throw a baseball on the fly from the mound to the plate but have lived a long time, have seen a lot, and have survived.

You might notice that young athletes and celebrities spend a lot of time talking about themselves, what they've done and plan to do. Often they're quite cocky, especially if they've seen a lot of success. But older people have evolved beyond the self-centeredness of youth. They've lived long enough to learn what's really important in life and to realize how blessed they are. And boy, do they have some wonderful stories!

Almost every person on the homestretch of life has enough wonderful stories to fill a book. Hilarious stories, sad stories, dramatic stories. And they love telling them! Or they *would* love telling them if anyone ever sat still long enough to listen. If you decided to sit still long enough to listen, you would be giving a great gift to that older person, but you would also be giving a great gift to yourself. It's the old story, as old as time, it seems. You go out to be a blessing to someone else, and you end up getting the bigger blessing.

I, for one, am glad I am not the Lone Ranger when it comes to aging. I'm glad there are other people walking this road with me. Sometimes I need to look down and see their footprints so I will know where to go. Sometimes I need to reach out my hand and help someone along who is struggling. And always I need to hear what they have to say, for when people speak from experience, they almost always speak great wisdom.

CHAPTER 9

PAY ATTENTION TO DETAILS

Details make perfection, and perfection is not a detail.

—LEONARDO DA VINCI, ARTIST AND SCIENTIST

One of the great privileges of my life was getting to know John Wooden. Coach Wooden was the greatest basketball coach—and possibly the greatest coach in any sport—who ever lived. Over a forty-year career, his teams won 885 games and lost just 203. But even more impressive are his ten national championships. Today if a coach wins two national championships, we call him a Hall of Famer. Imagine winning ten!

One day I was interviewing Coach Wooden for a book and asked him a simple question but one that I love to ask of anyone who has been extraordinarily successful: "If you could pinpoint just one secret of success in life, what would it be?" He thought for a moment and finally said, "The closest I have ever come to one secret of success is this: a lot of little things done well."

This answer meshed perfectly with something he once wrote.

High performance and production are achieved only through the identification and perfection of small but relevant details—little things done well … I derived great satisfaction from identifying and perfecting those "trivial" and often troublesome details, because I knew, without doubt, that each one brought UCLA a bit closer to our goal: competitive greatness. If you collect enough pennies you'll eventually be rich. Each relevant and perfect detail was another penny in our bank.[11]

Notice his choice of words in that first sentence: "small but relevant details." One of the greatest lessons you can learn in life is that details, though small, can be very relevant. Free throw shooting, for example, is considered a detail in the game of basketball. There's only one person involved, there's no dribbling or passing involved, no one is guarding the shooter, and the clock is stopped. Players spend much more time practicing their three-pointers than their free throws because three-pointers seem much more important to the outcome of the game. But if you know basketball, you know that fans and coaches often lament that a game was lost at the free throw line. When you lose by three points but missed five free throws, you realize what a "small but relevant detail" free throw shooting is.

Here are some "small but relevant details" that, if you pay close attention to them as you age, will make you happier on the homestretch.

First, take your medicine. Did you know that 90 percent of seniors takes at least one prescription and 80 percent takes two? And did you

---

11   John Wooden and Steve Jamison, *Wooden on Leadership: How to Create a Winning Organization* (New York: McGraw-Hill, 2005), 135–136.

know 55 percent of seniors don't take their medication properly?[12] There are lots of reasons for this, including poor memory, cost, the fear of side effects, and simply not feeling like they need it. Sadly, when you see a senior being rushed to the hospital, it's often because they failed to take important medication.

Taking your medicine takes less than a minute of your time. That's what qualifies it as a detail. It's not some big project that you have to carve out space for in your day. But if you don't do it, it could profoundly affect how you feel—or even whether you get to go on living. So take your medicine! If you need to create a system to help you remember, such as setting a daily alarm or having a family member double-check with you each day, do it!

Second, exercise your mind. I carry a book with me everywhere I go. And I do mean everywhere. When I was working for the Orlando Magic, I held a book while I watched the games so I could read a page or two during the time-outs. All the pounding music and flashing lights and team mascot Stuff carrying on his antics at center court didn't faze me. I truly believe this is one of the biggest reasons why I am still writing books in my eighties. I may not be able to run marathons like I used to, but my mind is as sharp as ever because I have exercised it like crazy.

As we age, our brains shrink, and the blood circulation slows, which causes a loss of some nerve cell connections. You experience the effect of this when you have a memory lapse or a moment of confusion. Many people think, "I wonder if I'm getting dementia." But in the vast majority of cases, the answer is no. You're just experiencing the normal effects of aging.

---

12   MediPENSE, "Top 10 Reasons Seniors Do Not Take Their Medications," accessed February 17, 2023, https://medipense.com/
top-10-reasons-seniors-do-not-take-their-medications/.

The good news is that you can slow these symptoms by exercising your brain. For example, learning a new skill such as painting or playing the piano forces your brain to wake up and stay active. Working puzzles or playing games that involve math or strategy also help. And of course, reading, especially if you read books that challenge your mind.

Exercising your mind is like taking your medicine in the sense that it doesn't take a lot of time or effort. In fact, sitting down with a good book or working a few puzzles can be relaxing and enjoyable.

Third, make a plan. Not long ago I met my writer and good friend, Mark Atteberry, at the Tap Room at Dubsdread in Orlando for lunch. We had already discussed doing this book as our next project and were going to discuss it further. But before we started, I whipped out two sheets of paper and handed them to Mark. It was a typewritten list of forty-four book ideas I still want to do. Knowing me as well as he does, Mark was not surprised.

> One of the biggest problems with older people—and the reason so many of them just kind of fade into oblivion before they die—is that they stop planning for tomorrow.

One of the biggest problems with older people—and the reason so many of them just kind of fade into oblivion before they die—is that they stop planning for tomorrow. I'm not suggesting that everybody ought to be planning a book to write. But I am saying that you ought to be planning *something*. Is there a trip you want to take? An improvement you want to make to your house? A new neighbor you should get to know? A family member who needs encouragement? An old friend you'd like to reconnect with? It doesn't have to be something big. Depending on your health, maybe it can't be something big. But thinking about something you want to do tomorrow gives you a reason to be engaged and excited. Above all, it gives you a reason to get out of bed in the morning with a sense of purpose!

When Coach Wooden passed away, one of his former players, Andre McCarter, wrote a tribute to him in which he commented on Coach's constant attention to detail. He wrote, "Coach taught us how to put on our socks; no wrinkles in the socks meant no blisters on the feet. The practical application of wrinkle free socks is the equivalent to Song of Solomon 2:15. The Word says to identify and deconstruct the little foxes that will spoil the vine. This is a powerful principle in maintaining a healthy marriage, business relationships, and sports teams."

Socks.

Wrinkles.

Blisters.

Small but relevant details.

Pay attention to them if you want to be happy on the homestretch.

CHAPTER 10

LAUGH AT YOUR SENIOR MOMENTS

Call it a "senior moment" and you can get
away with pretty much anything.

—GREETING CARD SAYING

An older married couple realized they were having a hard time remembering things, so they agreed that, going forward, they would write everything down. That evening, while watching TV, the wife asked her husband if he would get her a bowl of ice cream. He said he would and got up out of his chair. As he started for the kitchen, his wife said, "Wait a minute. Remember what we talked about? Don't you think you should write it down?"

Her husband said, "It's just a bowl of ice cream. I think I can remember that."

She said, "But I want chocolate syrup and sprinkles and nuts on it. I really think you should write it down. You know how forgetful you are." But he assured her that he would have no trouble fulfilling her request.

Sometime later the man returned to his wife with a plate of fried eggs, bacon, and toast. His wife looked at him and shook her head. "I knew you would mess things up if you didn't write it down. I told you I wanted my eggs scrambled!"

Senior moments are as much a part of aging as aches and pains. In fact, they may be *more* a part of aging because there are painkillers you can take for the aches and pains but not much you can do to fix senior moments. I've met a lot of people who are embarrassed by their senior moments. They see them as a sign of decline, proof positive that they are either over the hill or mighty close to it. If you're one of those people, I have good news for you. According to an article in the *Wall Street Journal*,[13] research shows that cognitive abilities change as we age but not necessarily in the way you think.

It works like this. When we are in our twenties, what's called "fluid intelligence"—things such as short-term memory and processing speed—hit their peak and then slowly start to decline, picking up speed as we age. This is why as you work your way into your fifties and sixties and beyond, you find it harder and harder to call up the names of people you know very well. If you take a minute and think hard, you can come up with it. But it doesn't flash into your mind as fast as it once did. It's also why you can walk into a room and forget for a moment what you were intending to do. You'll think of it if you stand there for a moment, but it's an effort.

However, here's the good news, the surprising part: What's called "crystallized intelligence" does not appreciably decline throughout

---

13 Alison Gopnik, "The Cognitive Advantages of Growing Older," Wall Street Journal, November 2018, February 17, 2023, https://www.wsj.com/articles/the-cognitive-advantages-of-growing-older-1541170622.

our lives. Crystallized intelligence encompasses the things we have learned or, you could say, our depth of knowledge. For example, if you learned how to play the piano in your twenties, you're not going to slowly forget how as you age. Eubie Blake, the legendary pianist and composer, was performing right up until the time of his death at age ninety-six. People also don't forget how to write or read or speak or cook or a hundred other things. You also don't forget things like your relationship with God or the tenets of your faith. People in their eighties and nineties who can't remember why they got up and walked to the kitchen can tell you all about Jesus and why they love him.

Do you see what good news this is? God has designed us not to forget the important stuff! Who cares if you can't recall a name? That's such a common occurrence that medical professionals don't even count it when giving memory tests. And what does it matter if you go to the kitchen to get a glass of water and end up with an ice cream bar? Doesn't that make life more interesting? The big thing to be thankful for is that you won't forget the big stuff.

So let me offer two suggestions for coping with those senior moments.

First, don't let them worry you.

Look at it this way. The whole world is having senior moments. If you were the only one, maybe some serious concern would be justified, but you aren't. And besides, what good did worrying about something ever do you? Remember this little verse:

Worry never climbed a hill
Worry never paid a bill
Worry never dried a tear
Worry never calmed a fear
Worry never darned a heel
Worry never cooked a meal

Worry never led a horse to water

Worry never done a thing you'd think it oughta.

Second, don't let your senior moments embarrass you.

I realize that some people are more self-conscious than others. It takes almost nothing to cause some people to turn bright red. If you're such a person, there's probably nothing I can say to change you. But if you're just a person who feels embarrassed when you have a senior moment, relax. Learn to laugh at yourself. Here are three benefits of laughing at yourself.

> Laughing at yourself means you know you're a mess like the rest of us—and you admit it.

One, laughing at yourself endears you to people. They will see your senior moment and maybe feel a moment of tension as they wait for your reaction. When you break out in laughter or make a joke about it, they will relax and feel a rush of good feelings toward you.

Two, laughing at yourself lets people know you're authentic. One of the main reasons why some people have a hard time laughing at themselves is because their ego demands that they try to give off the image of infallibility. They want you to think they never make a mistake, that they are totally on the ball every minute. Laughing at yourself means you know you're a mess like the rest of us—and you admit it. Authenticity is one of the most attractive qualities a person can have.

Three, laughing at yourself separates you from your performance. So many people in this world are judged according to how they perform in their job, as a parent, or in their spiritual lives. This is not good. We are all much, much more than what we do and how well we do it. Laughing at yourself reminds people of this. Laughing at yourself says, "Yes, I made a silly mistake, but it doesn't change who I am!"

Let me add one word of caution about laughing at yourself, however. Simple senior moments—the silly things we do—should be laughed at. But if you're laughing when you feel like crying, if you're covering up depression or dark, desperate thoughts with forced laughter, you probably need to talk to someone who can help you sort out those feelings. I am not a doctor, and I am not dispensing medical advice. But I know laughter is great therapy for senior moments and terrible therapy for deeper emotional problems.

I'll leave you with a quote from Mark Twain: "Humor is the great thing, the saving thing after all. The minute it crops up, all our hardnesses yield, all our irritations, and resentments flit away, and a sunny spirit takes their place."

CHAPTER 11

BE CAREFUL

The rate of deaths after falls is rising for people over 75.[14]

—KATIE HAFNER, NEW YORK TIMES

On October 25, 2022, I met my writer, Mark Atteberry, for lunch to discuss this book for the first time. I had scratched out some notes and was anxious to share them with him, but in a classic senior moment, I forgot and left them in the car. When I returned to the car, I retrieved the notes, closed and locked the door, and then turned and fell flat on my face. I've stepped up on thousands, perhaps millions, of curbs in my life without incident, but this one got me—and left a mark. I had a nice two-inch gash just below my elbow.

A very sweet server saw my tumble and took charge. She led me back to the table where Mark, who didn't know what had happened, was waiting and then brought out a wet towel and cleaned me up before placing a bandage she had rummaged from a coworker's purse

---

14   Katie Hafner, "Deadly Falls in Older Americans Are Rising. Here's How to Prevent Them," *New York Times*, June 4, 2019, A16.

over the wound. She fussed over me like a mother would her three-year-old. I was very grateful for her kindness.

When she left the table, I told Mark what happened and why. I have neuropathy in my feet, and sometimes I can't feel them. They don't exactly hurt, but sometimes it feels like I have two big blocks of wood at the end of my legs. So when I step up on a curb, for example, I can't always feel if I have placed my foot in the right spot. This time I wasn't looking down and couldn't feel that just my toes were on the curb. They slipped off when I shifted my weight, and I went *boom!*

I was grateful to God that I wasn't more seriously hurt. I was also embarrassed, not so much for falling but because people in my life who knew about my neuropathy had been encouraging me to use a cane, and I had stubbornly resisted. Like most people, I didn't want to make that concession to my age. It felt like a surrender of sorts, and I have never been one to surrender. I told myself that only decrepit people use a cane, and I am not decrepit. When I shared this with Mark, I didn't get much sympathy. He said, "Pat, it's time to use the cane."

He was right, of course.

There's something within all of us that makes us lie to ourselves, and most of those lies start with the words "You don't need to ..."

"You don't need to use a cane."

"You don't need to get a hearing aid."

"You don't need to take that medicine."

"You don't need to quit riding your bike."

"You don't need to ask someone to drive you."

"You don't need to pay someone to clean out the gutters."

As I was researching this book, I stumbled across a quote that has been attributed to many people: "You don't stop doing things because you get old. You get old because you stop doing things." Sounds good, doesn't it? Very pithy. But if you think about it for even a moment, you realize the statement has problems.

The truth is, there *does* come a time when you need to stop doing certain things. It's called being careful. Let me give you three guidelines on how to know when the time has come to make a change to your routine.

> The truth is, there *does* come a time when you need to stop doing certain things. It's called being careful.

A first way you can know it's time to make a change is when the people who know you best and love you most are telling you it's time. This will most likely be your family members or maybe a few close friends. I've seen older people get angry when this happens. "They're trying to take away my independence!" they say. Or "They're trying to take over my life!" Or "They're just trying to put me out to pasture!" These statements are almost never true. When your family members and loved ones encourage you to make one of these changes, it's because they love you and want what's best for you.

Here's something for you to think about. Anytime the people closest to you, the people who know you best and love you most, give you a piece of advice that stings, it's almost a certainty that you have a blind spot. That's actually where the sting is coming from. They see something you don't see.

Don't feel bad. People of all ages have blind spots. Sometimes when we get older, we have even more. The key to solving this situation is to listen without getting angry and ask yourself a simple question: "How many people are telling me this?" If only one person is saying it, maybe the time to make the change hasn't come yet. But if multiple people are in agreement, you can be pretty sure the time has come.

A second way you can know it's time to make a change is when you start having episodes. My spill on the sidewalk might as well have been a voice out of heaven, saying, "Pat, the old tootsies are not what they used to be. It's time to break out the cane." Sadly, I have known people who had to have multiple episodes before they finally admitted that they needed to make some changes.

And let me say this about episodes: one is all it takes to ruin—or even end—your life. I was blessed not to suffer any serious damage when I fell. But I could have landed in a way that slammed my head against the concrete. I could have torn up my knee or broken my leg. For older people, the difference between mild damage and serious damage is small, and serious damage takes much longer to heal.

And a third way you can know it's time to make a change is when you realize you're doing activities that no one else your age is doing. (If you happen to be Tom Brady, you can skip this point. Otherwise, read on.)

In the Orlando area, a pastor I know was driving down a busy four-lane road and passed one of his parishioners on a bicycle. The pastor was stunned and made it a point to look the man up the following Sunday at church. He said, "Stanley, I think it's great that you can still get out and ride your bike, but you're eighty-nine. I'm not sure it's a good idea at this point. All it would take is one mishap and you would be finished." Stanley, who loved and trusted his preacher, put his bike away for good.

There's a reason why you don't see eighty- and ninety-year-old people out riding bicycles. It's not because they can't ride them; it's because the risk is so great for a catastrophic injury if there's an accident.

But sometimes we take pride in being the oldest. One gentleman, at sixty-seven, loved to tell people he was the oldest guy on his softball team. And it wasn't a senior's team; he was playing with twenty- and thirty-year-olds. Naturally, he was the pitcher because it was the only position that didn't require him to run around or throw the ball hard. The problem was that his reflexes had been slowed by age, and one night a muscle-bound thirty-year-old hit a hot smash back through the box and just about killed him because he couldn't get his glove up fast enough to protect himself.

Look around.

Are you the oldest person—or among the oldest people—doing an activity that is traditionally something younger people do? That might be a reason to be proud. It might also be a wake-up call. You need to be careful.

And here's the thing about being careful: it doesn't always have to involve quitting. A tennis player can switch to pickleball. A softball player who needs to quit playing can become a coach. A person who should no longer get up on a ladder and clean out the gutters can still work in the flower beds. A person who needs to quit driving at night can still drive during the daytime. The point is not to become a couch potato, but to craft a life that fits who you are today, a life that provides a nice balance between activity and common sense.

CHAPTER 12

FOCUS ON WHAT YOU CAN DO, NOT ON WHAT YOU CAN'T

Focus is a matter of deciding what you're not going to do.

—JOHN CARMACK, COMPUTER PROGRAMMER

Aging has its pluses and minuses. On the minus side is the realization that there are things we can't do anymore.

For example, when you're young, or even middle-aged, the idea of spending a long day at a theme park with your family is exciting. When you get older, not so much. Instead of picturing yourself gliding through the air on some newfangled thrill ride, you imagine yourself sitting on a bench, nursing your aching back and feet, while the rest of the family enjoys the ride. Or when your gutters are full of leaves, you have a flashback to a time when you would get up there and clean them out with no problem. Now you're not sure you could carry the ladder around the house. But even if you could, you know your shaky balance would make climbing up there an insane decision. So you call a handyman and feel a little sadness even as you punch in the number.

Maybe, even as you read this book, you're depressed by all the items you've had to add to your "can't do anymore" list. Perhaps you're a lifelong golfer whose ailing back just won't let you play anymore. Or maybe your children have recently informed you that they're taking your keys and that you will no longer be allowed to drive. I've never heard of anyone taking *that* well.

Even if you're not quite there yet, the day is coming. So let me offer some advice because I have been there for a while and had some time to think about it. There are three facts I'd like for you to think about.

First, throughout your life there have always been things you couldn't do. When you were a kid, your parents wouldn't let you play in the street or stay home from school whenever you wanted or have donuts for dinner or slug your annoying brother. Then when you went to school, they wouldn't let you skip the classes you didn't like or pay the smartest kid in the class to do your homework for you. When you got a job, they wouldn't let you clock in and out whenever you wanted or take two-hour lunches. Then when you finally started building your career and making some money, the government wouldn't let you opt out of paying taxes.

You can't name a time in your life when you were completely free of restrictions. And what did you do when restrictions were imposed on you? You adjusted. You didn't necessarily like it, but you adjusted.

Visit any day care center or church nursery when a child is being checked in for the first time. More than likely you'll see that child throw an absolute fit, crying and clinging to his mother in an effort to change her mind about leaving him there. The next morning you'll see the same routine, and maybe the morning after that, and the morning after that. The child is fighting reality, tooth and nail. But at some point, the child understands it's a losing battle and decides his life will be much better if he just accepts what he can't change.

That's what you need to do. Instead of whining and moaning about the things you can no longer do, accept reality, and make peace with the situation. It is not an overstatement to say that your ability to do this will go a long way toward determining your happiness. If you doubt this, think about the unhappiest people you know. I'm guessing they'll all have at least one unchangeable reality they're futilely fighting against that they need to accept and embrace.

> Instead of whining and moaning about the things you can no longer do, accept reality, and make peace with the situation.

Second, always remember that, while there are things you can no longer do, there are other things you do better than ever. This is the fact that often slips through the cracks in our thinking. The abilities we lose get so much of our attention that we seldom think about the abilities we don't lose.

Wight Martindale, a college history professor who was still teaching at the age of eighty-three, had an interesting perspective on his job. He knew that most people saw him as too old to connect with college students, but he argued that his age gave him a unique perspective on history, an understanding of it that a much younger professor couldn't possibly have. He said, "Younger people ... should be running things today because tomorrow is their concern, not mine. Teaching history and literature, on the other hand, begins with perspective—something older people should be good at."[15]

---

15   Wight Martindale, "This Old Man, He Teaches History," *Wall Street Journal*, November 16, 2022, A17.

In 2022 the Houston Astros won the World Series. Their manager, Dusty Baker, is a perfect example of how some abilities diminish and others increase as we age. In the 1970s Dusty was a top-flight major league outfielder. His ability kept him in the majors for nineteen years and enabled him to rack up some very nice career stats, including 1,981 hits and 242 home runs. He even hit behind Hank Aaron in the lineup on the day Aaron hit home run number 715 to break Babe Ruth's record.

Today Dusty is in his seventies. His chances of hitting a Major League fastball are slim and none. And if he did hit one, he'd probably need the bullpen cart to haul him around the bases. But while his physical skills are gone, his knowledge of the game and experience are off the charts. You couldn't dream up a situation he hasn't seen. A young manager will run into situations that are new but not Dusty. He's seen it all, which gives his team a tremendous advantage.

Third, understand that while there are things you can no longer do, there are many new things you could learn to do. In 2017 a book of George W. Bush's oil painting portraits of sixty-six physically or mentally wounded U.S. soldiers was published. In 2021 he released a second book of paintings, this time of forty-three immigrants that he found particularly inspiring. Most people are surprised to learn that Bush didn't start painting until he left the presidency in 2009. He suddenly had time on his hands and wondered what he could do with it. An essay about painting, written by Winston Churchill, sparked his interest, and he thought, "Why not give it a try?"

What new thing could you learn to do?

You might read about Mr. Bush's paintings and say, "But I'm no painter. I've never painted anything in my life." Neither had he!

But if painting doesn't interest you, perhaps you could start taking piano lessons. Did you know that playing piano stimulates the brain and improves your memory? Or what about photography? Or if not photography, maybe there's a book in you that needs to be written. Don't say you're too old to start writing. Laura Ingalls Wilder of *Little House on the Prairie* fame didn't get her first book published until she was sixty-five. But she was a mere child compared with Lorna Page, whose first book, *A Dangerous Weakness*, was published when she was ninety-three!

It's hard to see and feel our abilities slipping away. But there's no reason to sit and brood about it. You still have other abilities and can develop new ones. You'll be happier on the homestretch if you focus on what you *can* do and not on what you can't.

CHAPTER 13

LIVE WHAT YOU'VE LEARNED

Life is a grindstone. Whether it grinds us
down or polishes us up depends on us.

—THOMAS L. HOLDCROFT, AUTHOR AND THEOLOGIAN

Around 350 BC, Aristotle wrote about things we could only learn by doing. Today we call it experiential learning or learning by experiencing. It is, however, not the only way to learn. Rote learning is when you memorize the information, much the way we did our multiplication tables when we were kids. And then there's didactic learning, where you sit and listen to an instructor explain things. Most of us have learned things in all three of these ways. In this chapter I want to focus on the things we learn by experience.

I remember the time I gave a speech to a *Fortune* 500 company. They told me I had thirty minutes, which was shorter than most corporate events required and therefore shorter than I was accustomed to speaking. I remember thinking that it wouldn't matter if I went a little overtime. I didn't want to cut out any of my speech, and after all, don't most speakers stretch the time limit a little?

So I walked up on the stage and did my thing. I gave the whole speech and went about fifteen minutes longer than they had asked me to speak. When I came down off the stage, I was met by one of the organizers of the event and told that I would never be asked to speak to the company again because I had not respected the instructions I'd been given. He told me that because I went long, other speakers and events that had been planned would have to be cut short or eliminated. He was not happy, and I was embarrassed.

Would you like to guess what I did the next time I was given a specific time limit for my speech? I don't suppose there was ever a speaker in all of history who was more conscious of the time than I was!

You live and learn.

But here's the big question: do you then live *what* you learn?

Often people don't.

Occasionally, I'll read about someone who's been married four or five times. Or someone who's had his license revoked because he's gotten so many speeding tickets. Or someone who's been let go from multiple jobs for the same offense. Or someone who's had multiple affairs. Or someone who's had serious health problems but never changed his unhealthy lifestyle. And I think, "How does this happen?" Surely these people are not so dense that they don't realize they're doing things wrong. Surely they realize they've messed up repeatedly. Of course, they do. The problem is, they're not living what they've learned.

Here are two pieces of advice that will help you learn and benefit from your mistakes.

First, admit that your mistakes are indeed your *mistakes.* This is where it all goes wrong for a lot of people. They have a terrible experience, but they learn nothing from it because they are too busy blaming other people or things.

Sadly, blaming others has become an art form in our culture. We do it with even the simplest things, such as when you're walking down the street and trip, then immediately turn and look at the sidewalk as if it was responsible. Never mind that you were texting as you were walking.

> It's not until you stand up and start taking responsibility for your actions that you become your own person again.

But it's the big things that are the problem. Experts say that blaming others for our mistakes and problems is an attractive choice for a lot of people because it puts ownership of the problem and therefore the responsibility for fixing it on someone else. That might feel good in the moment, but if you fall into the habit of always blaming others, you eventually lose any sense of autonomy in your life. You program yourself to think and act like a puppet that is always being controlled by others. It's not until you stand up and start taking responsibility for your actions that you become your own person again.

Second, learn to reflect on the things that happen to you. Do you remember the closing scene of the movie *Gone with the Wind?* A dashing Rhett Butler has just walked out on Scarlett O'Hara, informing her in very raw terms that he doesn't care where she goes or what she does. The music swells, and poor Scarlett, with tears streaming down her face, says, "I can't let him go. I can't. There must be some way to bring him back. But I can't think about this now. I'll go crazy if I do. I'll think about it tomorrow."

There are times when thinking about a problem tomorrow is a good choice. Sometimes our emotions are too tender and our wounds are too deep to think objectively in the moment. However, when one tomorrow turns into two, and two turn into three, and before long a week or a month has gone by and you're still not facing what happened, you're effectively crippling your chances of learning something positive from your experience.

Why is the I'll-think-about-it-tomorrow approach to problems so common?

One reason is because it keeps us from having to face something about ourselves that is painful. Our culpability, for example. Or maybe something unfortunate we said or did that made an already difficult situation worse. Perhaps the fire was already burning because of someone else's actions, but then you came along and poured gasoline on it.

A second reason we put off thinking about a problem is because it keeps us from having to face things about other people that are painful. Like that person we love to blame everything on. Maybe they aren't really the villain after all, which is frustrating because we need a villain. We *want* a villain! Have you ever been in a situation where you learned someone was innocent and it bothered you because it was so much more convenient when you could tell everybody he was guilty?

Since self-reflection is so important to learning life's lessons, here are a couple of suggestions to make it easier for you.

One is to make it part of a daily quiet time. Do you set aside time for Bible reading or prayer? If so, include a few minutes of self-reflection. Think about what happened to you that day, good or bad, and ask yourself why it happened. Or think about the choices you made, and determine if they were wise or foolish.

Second is to write your thoughts down. Some people rebel at the thought of keeping a diary, but the advantage is this: you can go back and review what you've written in recent weeks or months and see if you've progressed or regressed. Are you still reacting to a certain problem the same way? Have you softened? Are your thoughts and emotions healthier than they once were? Seeing progress can bring great encouragement.

I've always felt that there's nothing more pitiful than an older person who is still making the mistakes of their youth. It's one thing to make a mistake when you're twenty-five; it's another to make the same mistake when you're fifty-five. Don't let it happen. Learn from your mistakes, and then live what you've learned.

CHAPTER 14

COME UP WITH SOME NEW DEFINITIONS

True life is lived when tiny changes occur.

—LEO TOLSTOY, AUTHOR

Did you know that how you define certain words will determine the quality and direction of your life? Let me give you a few examples.

Blessings. If you define blessings purely in monetary or materialistic terms, you're going to overlook many of the wonderful things in your life that have value beyond the physical realm, such as friendship, good health, and peace of mind. And you will spend all of your time chasing material things at the expense of life's richer gifts. It's been said that the person most to be pitied in this world is the man who can't see beyond a dollar sign.

Marriage. If you define marriage as a relationship that is designed to meet your needs and make you happy, you are going to be selfish and demanding with your spouse—and probably divorced.

Christian. If you define being a Christian as simply going to church for an hour on Sunday, you will give little or no thought to your relationship with God the rest of the time. You may learn to say and do what's necessary to be accepted in the church community, but your actual faith will be an empty shell.

I could go on, but you get the idea. The definition of a word is like the rudder of a ship. It steers you here or there, into good or bad choices and, ultimately, into calm or troubled waters.

I have found as I have aged that it's necessary to rethink some definitions. Let me share some words I've had to redefine.

Responsibility. I was a sports executive for over fifty years. Four NBA franchises (the 76ers, Bulls, Hawks, and Magic) made me their general manager, which means they handed me the keys to the car. I was the guy who signed players and made trades, which in sports is the number one determining factor in the team's success. I drafted Charles Barkley in 1984 and Shaquille O'Neal in 1992, traded for Dr. J, and traded away Pistol Pete Maravich and Moses Malone, to name just a few of the moves I made. Talk about a huge responsibility! Don't think I didn't sweat bullets over some of those decisions.

But things are different now.

I am no longer responsible for the fate of a professional sports franchise. I no longer make decisions that involve millions of dollars. I don't hold the happiness of an entire fan base in my hands. For me today, responsibility is a much simpler thing. A smaller thing in some ways but no less important. At this point my number one responsibility is simply to finish well. I need to keep from making a foolish mistake that would tarnish my name. I need to make sure all of my relationships are healthy and strong. And I need to stay close to God, the one I am going to stand before when the final buzzer sounds on my life.

It's true that the phone doesn't ring like it once did. No player agents are trying to woo me. I don't find myself in front of a camera as often as I once did. But make no mistake, I still have important responsibilities; you just won't hear about them on ESPN.

Success. I own something that is considered the ultimate symbol of success in my profession: my Philadelphia 76ers NBA championship ring from 1983. I remember the night we won it all. The joy and elation are impossible to describe. You've seen such celebrations on TV, I'm sure. I can assure you that the excitement is as real as it looks.

You might think that I wear my championship ring when I go to a major function or at least keep it on display in my home so I can show it off to visitors. I don't. In fact, it's put away, and I never bring it out. To be honest I never even think about it. The reason is because it represents yesterday, and I am not a yesterday person; I am a today and tomorrow person. Also, while the ring represents success, it's old news. Even devoted sports fans would have a hard time telling you who won the NBA title in 1983. Most of them don't know and don't care. Simply put, success for me is something very different at this point in my life. It's so much simpler, so much more basic, and it has nothing to do with rings.

Now in my eighties, success for me means staying healthy—following my doctor's instructions and staying cancer-free. It means being a good husband to Ruth and being a mentor and cheerleader for my nineteen children and twenty-one grandkids. It means going to church and being a good witness for Christ. It means reading good books and sketching out ideas for more books I want to write. It even means something as simple as settling back in my easy chair and watching a big game on television.

For me, success is no longer something I have to chase. It's not out there hiding somewhere in the wild. It's right in front of me and all around me in the simple things I do every day. No, it's not as glamorous as the success I used to chase, but it's just as meaningful and maybe more so.

Values. I heard a story about an artist whose paintings were on display and for sale at a local gallery. He asked the gallery owner if anyone had shown interest in buying any of his paintings. The owner said, "I have good news and bad news. The good news is that someone came in and asked if I thought your paintings would appreciate in value after your death. I said yes, and he immediately bought all of your paintings."

The artist said, "That's wonderful! What's the bad news?"

The gallery owner said, "The man was your doctor."

Death is always a real possibility, of course. But there comes a point in our lives where we can sense it sitting out there on the horizon, waiting to make its move. We know our years are dwindling, that we're on the homestretch of life, and it changes the way we think. Things that at one time were not very important to us suddenly are. Things that at one time rarely crossed our minds are suddenly front and center.

I experienced this when I was diagnosed with multiple myeloma. It was very much like being told that there's an assassin out to get you and that he just got off the afternoon bus two blocks from your house. My list of priorities was suddenly in flux. Things that had been at the top, such as career success, slid down several notches. And things that I had been taking somewhat for granted, such as my relationships (including my relationship with God), shot straight to the top. My whole life felt like a snow globe that someone had picked up and shaken, and I was suddenly scrambling to reorient myself.

If this sounds like a bad thing, think again. Most of us *need* to rethink our priorities. Too many people sail through their younger and middle age years without giving a thought to their values. If realizing that death is lurking out there just beyond the horizon causes us to recalibrate, we should be thankful.

I'll close this chapter by encouraging you to come up with some new definitions to key words in your own life. Words you may have been using for years but that no longer mean what they used to because you've entered the homestretch of your life. You'll find that this exercise will help you find rest and peace. It will free you from having to chase ideas and concepts that are no longer relevant. It will allow you to relax and be who you have become instead of trying to still be who you once were.

> Most of us *need* to rethink our priorities. Too many people sail through their younger and middle age years without giving a thought to their values.

CHAPTER 15

MANAGE YOUR WORRIES WISELY

You can't stop the waves, but you can learn to surf.

—JON KABAT-ZINN, PROFESSOR OF MEDICINE

As the old saying goes, I have good news and bad news.

The good news is that, as you age, certain worries drop off your radar. Worries like choosing a career, finding a job, marrying the right person, raising your kids, and getting them through college are in your rearview mirror because those issues have been resolved. There's also the fact that, as you reach the homestretch of life, certain things become less important to you and therefore less worrisome. A good example would be the constant advances in technology. Once you retire and leave the workforce, the pressure to keep up with each new advancement decreases, allowing you to settle in with what you feel comfortable with and forget about the rest. A recent survey indicated that over half of people fifty-five and older had never heard of the metaverse, and of those who had heard of it, 45 percent said they weren't interested.[16]

The bad news is that older people still have plenty of things to worry about because some worries are unique to older people. For example, people in their thirties and forties never think about having to move into a nursing home. People in their fifties and sixties might give it some thought as they care for their elderly parents. But people in their seventies and eighties think about it a lot, especially if they have health challenges and no family to take care of them. And most find the idea of living in a nursing home terrifying.

Another worry that is common to older people is that their health will begin to deteriorate. We all know that our bodies are going to wear out eventually. We also know diseases such as cancer, diabetes, heart disease, and Alzheimer's afflict millions of people. What we *don't* know is what's coming for us or when. I can attest to the fact that you can be planning to run a marathon early in the week and be sitting in a doctor's office getting a life-threatening diagnosis by the weekend. When we are young, random aches and pains barely get our attention. But when we get into our sixties and seventies, random aches and pains can be frightening. When they strike, we immediately wonder if it's something serious.

A third worry that is especially heavy for older people is running out of money. Even if we have put money away, we still wonder if we have enough to last until we die. Recent statistics show that almost

---

16   Richard Eisenberg, "For Older Adults: A Hitchhiker's Guide
      To The Metaverse, Forbes, April 2022, February 17, 2023,
      https://www.forbes.com/sites/nextavenue/2022/04/15/
      for-older-adults-a-hitchhikers-guide-to-the-metaverse/?sh=fc7ae8d3477f.

half of Americans die broke.[17] This is a particularly terrifying thought because we've all heard horror stories about people who are forced to spend their last days in low-end nursing facilities that provide substandard care simply because they have no money. If you've ever been in such a place to visit a friend, if you've smelled the odor and seen the dirty floors and the disgusting-looking food, you will shudder at the thought of living there yourself—and worry about it a lot.

So people on the homestretch of life often trade one set of worries for another, which begs the question, which is worse, young people's worries or older people's worries? My answer is that all worries are bad. Here are a few thoughts that will help you manage yours.

> There are many things we can influence but few things we can control.

First, don't worry about what you can't control. The key to grasping this idea is to understand the difference between influence and control. There are many things we can influence but few things we can control. For example, you can teach your children right from wrong and instill good values in them. That's influence. But you can't control what they do when they go out on their own.

I strongly recommend that you spend some time examining your worries.

Back in 1965, when I was the twenty-four-year-old general manager of the Spartanburg Phillies, I worried myself sick about two things: the weather and player moves that were made by executives higher up the food chain. One day the owner of the team, Mr. R. E. Littlejohn, said to me, "Pat, you're not going to last the season if you

---

17   Maurie Backman, "Almost half of Americans Die Nearly Broke," The Motley Fool, May 2017, February 17, 2023, https://www.fool.com/retirement/2017/05/30/almost-half-of-americans-die-nearly-broke.aspx.

don't quit worrying about every little thing. How much control do you have over the weather?"

"None," I answered.

He said, "And how much control do you have over player moves made by the Phillies brass?"

"None," I answered.

He said, "Okay, how much control do you have over how hot the hot dogs are and how cold the drinks are and how clean the restrooms are?"

"A lot," I answered.

He said, "Okay. Seems to me like you ought to worry about the things you can control and let the rest of it go."

Maybe it sounds crazy, but that advice may have saved my life—or at least saved me a bunch of ulcers.

Itemize your worries and ask yourself which ones you can influence and which ones are beyond your control. If you can influence a situation, by all means do it—within reason. I add this caveat because sometimes our efforts to influence go too far. Nagging, for example, is an effort to influence but will drive a wedge into your relationships. Smothering is also often rationalized as an effort to provide influence but only builds resentment. So yes, influence, but be smart about it.

But when you come to a situation that you can't influence or control, let it go. There's absolutely nothing positive that can come from you sitting around worrying about it.

Second, fight worry with activity. One thing worriers often do that is counterproductive is sit around and think. And think. And think some more. And often this thinking involves envisioning disaster scenarios. We picture the worst possible outcomes for the situation that is on our minds. Or we replay a conversation over and over and imagine hidden meanings in the words we heard: "What did he really mean by that? Was he trying to tell me something? Should I be offended?"

The best way I've found to stop this unhelpful ruminating is to get up and do something constructive. It forces you to think about something else. Go pick up your grandkids and take them to get ice cream. Or if they live too far away, call them and have a chat. Or walk across the street and visit a neighbor. Or go to the market and pick up the ingredients for your favorite recipe and then make it and take it to a shut-in. It will be a wonderful gift for them and an opportunity to change the channel in your mind for you.

You've heard the saying, "Idle hands are the devil's playground." It's true. Inactivity is fertile soil where all of our worst thoughts grow like weeds.

Finally, practice the art of affirmation. I picked up this great idea from author Amy Morin. She says there are two phrases she often says to herself. One is "Make it happen." For example, if her mind says, "I hope things go okay at work today," she quickly responds, "No need to hope. Just make it happen." Such a statement is an affirmation that she is in control of her actions and therefore in control of many outcomes.

The other phrase is, "I can handle it." For example, if her mind says, "I hope he doesn't get mad when I tell him," she quickly responds, "I can handle it if he does." This statement affirms that she is not a slave to what other people do, that even if they behave in an unbecoming way, she can control herself and maintain her dignity.[18]

I love this! We often think that people who talk to themselves must be a little nutty but not in this case. Speaking truthful, empower-

---

[18]   Amy Morin, "6 Ways to Stop Worrying About Things You Can't Control," Inc., April 2017, February 17, 2023, https://www.inc.com/amy-morin/6-ways-to-stop-worrying-about-things-you-cant-control.html.

ing, motivating words to yourself in the face of worry and anxiety is a great way to keep your mind focused in the right direction.

I'll close with this thought.

As a Christian, I have found comfort in the wisdom of the Bible. One verse in particular that is helpful in worrisome situations is Psalm 94:19 (NIV). It says, "When anxiety was great within me, your consolation brought me joy." We think David wrote this psalm. He was certainly a guy with many worries. At one time there was even a price on his head, forcing him to hide out in a wilderness to keep from being assassinated! But he found consolation—and ultimately joy—in the Lord. I encourage you to take your worries to God. Lay them at his feet and let him handle them. Then get into his Word and let his promises give you comfort.

CHAPTER 16

GO TO CHURCH

The Bible knows nothing of solitary religion.

—JOHN WESLEY, EVANGELIST

I am a church guy. I am a member of First Baptist in Orlando and have been for many years. I co-taught a Sunday school class there for several years and enjoyed every minute of it. Going to church to worship God with family and friends is one of the highlights of my week.

But I know not everyone feels the same way.

I've noticed that people who don't go to church can be divided into four groups.

The first group is highly suspicious of the church. They're not believers and see the church as a big scam, a way for preachers to rake in a lot of money.

The second group is anti-church because at some point in the past, they were wounded in church. They were mistreated or got their feelings hurt in some way.

The third group includes those people who were not raised in church. Their parents or grandparents didn't go, so they have no connection to any church anywhere. It's not something they even think about.

And the fourth group would include all the believers who have been to church and never had a bad experience but simply got lazy and dropped out.

If you're not a churchgoer, I'm sure you fit into one of these groups. I'd like to ask you to set your feelings aside for the remainder of this chapter and consider some reasons why going to church makes sense for everybody but especially people who are on the homestretch of life.

First, the church exists simply to give to you. Pay no attention to the hard-core skeptics who claim the church is out to rip you off. That may be true in a few rare cases if you're talking about a cult or some sort of dishonest enterprise that calls itself a church, but in a normal Christ-centered church, it isn't true at all.

The average church is engaged in benevolent enterprises all year long. They give toys to underprivileged kids at Christmastime and provide clothing and food for the homeless, shelter for victims of domestic abuse, practical assistance to unwed mothers, and financial support to missionaries who have dedicated their lives to helping people in need. They also offer educational opportunities for all ages, summer camps for kids, counseling for people who are struggling, and fellowship opportunities for people who are lonely, including many activities for seniors. And they offer all of these services for free! Honestly, I have never understood people who accuse the church of taking. Any fair-minded observer can see that the church gives and gives and gives some more.

I'm not saying you should go to church simply to take what the church gives. That would be a very selfish attitude. But I do believe the giving, helping, supportive nature of the church should warm our hearts and make us feel inclined toward it instead of opposed to it.

Second, the church gives you an opportunity to use your gifts. One problem many seniors run into is feeling useless or bored after they retire. They think it will be so wonderful to escape the daily grind of the workplace that they've been in for so many years, and it is at first. But for many, it isn't long until they start getting itchy. They need something to do. According to Joblist, over 50 percent of retirees head back into the workforce. And 60 percent of those say they are doing so not for the money but because they need something to do.[19]

I can't think of a better place to find something to do than your local church. Remember all those services and ministries they offer that I just mentioned? They need people to pull it all off! People with all kinds of talents and abilities. Are you an organizer? They need you. Are you a bookkeeper? They need you. Are you good with people? They need you. Do you enjoy working with the elderly or with children? They need you. Are you a musician or a teacher? They need you.

Keep in mind that you will need to prove yourself and establish credibility. Most churches do not allow people to just walk in off the street and take over. But if you are willing to prove yourself and establish trust, you will be given real opportunities to use your gifts in ways that truly make a difference.

Third, the church will challenge you to think beyond this life. I have often thought that one reason why so many people are gloomy and depressed is because they have nothing to look forward to. Their lives are hard. They have problems and hardships to deal with every day,

---

19   Joblist, "Q2 2022 United States Job Market Report," Job Market Reports, July 2022, February 17, 2023, https://www.joblist.com/jobs-reports/q2-2022-united-states-job-market-report.

and it all just seems so hopeless. They wonder, what's the point of it all? The church offers an answer to that question, a positive answer that will help you see a purpose in the things that happen to you and give you a reason for living.

Simply put, the answer is that you are not a random accident of biology. You were created by God for a specific purpose, which is to have a personal relationship with him first and foremost and then within that relationship to accomplish something meaningful that glorifies him during your time on earth. In my many years of life, having met thousands and thousands of people, it's my observation that people who don't know God and who have no real purpose are the most unhappy. And that goes double for people who are on the homestretch of life. I can't imagine anything more depressing than living out your golden years with no purpose. When you're young, you can distract yourself with wild living and the pursuit of pleasure, but when those things fade away, what's left?

> You were created by God for a specific purpose, which is to have a personal relationship with him first and foremost and then within that relationship to accomplish something meaningful that glorifies him during your time on earth.

If you go to church, you will be constantly reminded of three things.

Your value. You are a one-of-a-kind creation of Almighty God.

Your future. If you are a Christian, you are saved and on your way to heaven.

Your purpose. You have a reason for living, and it is to serve God.

I know what you're thinking.

"But, Pat, what about all the people who get hurt in church? What about all the preachers who get caught having affairs? What about all the questionable financial practices? What about all the church splits? When I hear such stories, I feel like the church is something I need to stay away from!"

I understand. I've heard those stories too. So let me tell you how I have come to think about this.

For one thing, I learned a long time ago never to expect perfection from anything that involves humans. It's true that there are no perfect churches. Nor are there any perfect schools, agencies, businesses, or organizations of any kind. Isn't it a bit hypocritical to reject the church because it isn't perfect but then be involved with and supportive of other organizations that are equally imperfect, if not more so?

Also, the church is not as "messed up" as some people make it out to be. Yes, there are scandals. Yes, there are internal conflicts. But not as many as it seems. Keep in mind that just about any church scandal will make the front page of the paper, but a similar scandal happening at a restaurant or department store will never be known. The truth is, many churches are in such vibrant good health that you could attend for years and years and never encounter a problem. The key is to find a healthy church. Almost every community has them if you're willing to look.

Finally, even though I go to church and love the church, I don't worship the church. My faith doesn't depend on what the church does. If the church I attend had a big problem, I would be disappointed, yes, but my faith would remain strong because my faith is in God.

I believe the church offers far more pluses than minuses, far more blessings than dangers. Many on the homestretch of life have found it to be a wonderful source of comfort and hope.

CHAPTER 17

GET ALONG WITH YOUR FAMILY

—Happiness is having a large, loving, caring, close-knit family in another city.

—GEORGE BURNS, COMEDIAN

As you may know, I have a large family. As of this writing, the tally stands at nineteen kids and twenty-one grandkids. Christmas at our house is more like attending a convention than having a family get-together. But it's great. The challenges and adventures of those child-rearing years have now morphed into an unending supply of stories that make our times of reminiscing a real joy.

Unfortunately, many people on the homestretch of life are surprised to encounter challenges within the family. They assume that when they retire, they'll have more time to spend with kids and grandkids, which they believe will be just wonderful. They can't wait. What they fail to realize is that while *their* routine will change, the rest of the family's routines will not. Their kids will still be working,

103

and their grandkids will still be in school and involved with friends and extracurricular activities, leaving Grandma and Grandpa feeling a bit disappointed. "I thought we would spend more time together, but nothing has really changed" is a common refrain. Sometimes that disappointment can evolve into frustration or even resentment.

Here are some suggestions that will help you avoid family frustrations on the homestretch.

First, understand that the distance you sometimes feel between you and your kids and grandkids is normal and healthy. All the way back in the book of Genesis (2:24), God said that a man would leave his father and mother. He leaves not because of a strain between himself and his parents but because he has a wife, and the two of them will now create a family of their own.

But what does it mean to "leave" your father and mother? We know for sure that it's not a geographical thing. God doesn't stipulate a number of miles that should separate the parents and their children (although some space is surely a good thing). Rather, it's about what I would call "breathing room." Perhaps you've been in a relationship that felt smothering, where somebody was constantly crowding you. Every time you turned around, you bumped into them. Maybe they were always sticking their nose into your business or offering unsolicited advice or lecturing you for a choice you made. That kind of overbearing behavior coming from parents can drive a wedge between them and their children and create negative feelings.

And by the way, don't assume that smothering only happens when families live close together because it's not true. The world has shrunk dramatically because of technology. Even people who live hundreds of miles apart can see and text and talk to each other multiple times a day just as if they lived next door.

I know that sometimes breathing room is not what you want. You're retired now. You have more time on your hands and would love to be more involved in your kids' and grandkids' lives. But they don't call, they don't invite you to be involved in their lives, and you feel frustrated.

Relax.

They're busy and preoccupied with many things. Just because your phone isn't ringing every day doesn't mean they don't love you. It's far, far better to have breathing room—even if it's more than you want—than to have the tension that comes from being too close. I suspect that when you were the age of your kids, *your* parents felt the very same emotions you're struggling with right now as you went on with your busy life. It's a normal part of transitioning from one stage of life to another. Don't make it a bigger issue than it is.

Second, communicate well about things that create tension. There's an episode of *Everybody Loves Raymond* where Raymond's parents (who are their neighbors) get into the habit of just walking into Raymond's house without knocking. Of course, the obvious solution to this problem would be to lock the door, but that has not been their practice, and Raymond is afraid that if he starts locking the door, it will hurt his parents' feelings. Naturally—because the show is a comedy—there is the obligatory scene where Raymond and his wife are being affectionate on the couch when the door suddenly flies open, and Raymond's parents troop into the room. Eventually, Raymond has no choice but to be honest with his parents about their intrusive behavior.

I suspect a lot of people watch that episode and feel it hitting close to home. In many families there are tension-causing behaviors that need to be addressed but aren't. Maybe someone is constantly giving you unsolicited advice. Maybe someone is inappropriately nosy.

Maybe someone makes offhand comments that strike you as being critical. Maybe someone is always dropping in without calling first. The thing about little irritations is that they become major sources of anxiety, and even anger, if they aren't dealt with. The wise thing to do is meet them head-on. Speak kindly but clearly about your feelings and expectations. And be firm if you meet resistance. If you cave in and continue to allow the behavior that's driving you crazy, you will be forced to live, not only with that behavior but also with the knowledge that you wimped out and didn't fix the problem when you had the chance.

Third, disagree without being disagreeable. Politics and religion are two topics that can cause deep rifts in families and now more than ever. Politics in particular has evolved into a topic that produces real anger and animosity. I've heard many stories about families that have had blowups at the Thanksgiving or Christmas dinner table, resulting in close relatives not even wanting to speak to each other.

As one of the "elders" of the family, it's your job to set a good example. Even if you have strong feelings of your own on the subject at hand, it's your responsibility to hold your temper and even to play referee if others start getting hot under the collar. Be a calming influence. Change the subject. If you have to, say, "We're never going to settle this, so let's just talk about something else." Time with your family is too precious to spend your time arguing about issues that will never be settled to everyone's satisfaction.

Finally, be a blessing. If you overhear your married son talking about how he and his wife would love to paint a room in their house but just can't find the time to do it, why not volunteer? If you know that one of your grandkids needs to be taken to piano lessons after school on Thursdays, why not volunteer? If you sense that your kids need a weekend away without their children, why not volunteer to babysit so they can have that time? Not only will you be a great help, but you will also get the added blessings of feeling useful and spending extra time with your grandkids.

You might say, "But, Pat, I can't do those things because I live so far away." In that case, you need to be creative. What if you sent your kids a gift card so they could get away for a weekend? What if you took your tools and old clothes when you went for a visit so you could do a little handyman work around the house? What if you offered to pay for a household repair that you know your kids need but can't afford? There are always ways to be a blessing, no matter how far away you live.

> Time with your family is too precious to spend your time arguing about issues that will never be settled to everyone's satisfaction.

I feel genuinely sorry for the people I've known who had to face their homestretch years with the knowledge that their families were irreparably broken. I can think of few things more heartbreaking. Obviously, the happiness of your family doesn't depend entirely on you. But you can take it upon yourself to do everything in your power to keep the family strong and close-knit. It's an endeavor you will never regret.

CHAPTER 18

THINK ABOUT YOUR STUFF

Many possessions, if they do not make a man better,
are at least expected to make his children happier;
and this pathetic hope is behind many exertions.

—GEORGE SANTAYANA, PHILOSOPHER

Mark Atteberry was a pastor for forty-six years. During that time he officiated hundreds of funerals, and he tells me that a surprising number of those were marred by a family feud. He described one where two brothers and their families came together to bury their father. They hated each other so much that they refused to speak or even get near each other. They sat on opposite sides of the auditorium during the service and never acknowledged each other's presence.

On another day Mark was making final preparations for a service to begin when he heard angry shouting in the lobby of the church. He dropped what he was doing and ran to see what was happening. He found two brothers squared off with their dukes up, angry and shouting at each other, only seconds away from fisticuffs. He and one of the funeral directors stepped in between the brothers and calmed things down.

Mark says that in both of those cases, and several others like them, the anger was over the deceased person's estate. The "stuff" that was to be distributed to the heirs. Person A was feeling cheated and angry. Person B was angry that Person A was angry and unwilling to go with the flow. Cutting words were exchanged, and as is often the case, when words no longer seemed adequate to express anger, both parties were willing to resort to fists—even in the lobby of a church.

It goes without saying that people who are willing to mix it up in a church building have bigger issues than money, but let's set those aside and think about the trigger in both of these situations: the stuff.

Here's a principle that I believe is true most of the time: Dying is harder for people who have a lot of stuff. And even if it isn't harder for the person who's dying, it often is for their offspring. In the Bible, two of King David's sons—Absalom first and then Adonijah after Absalom was killed—grew impatient waiting for their father to die so they could inherit his kingdom and wealth. Both of them launched campaigns to speed things along. It got ugly, as you can imagine. I can't help thinking of how heartbroken a parent would be to see such things happening.

It's important to think about your stuff. Here are some things to consider.

First, everything you own is going to burn eventually. It really is just stuff, and for that reason it isn't worth having a family feud over. Always keep this in mind. Of course, you don't always have the final say in whether there will be a problem. If one of your family members has a disagreeable attitude and wants to cause a problem, there's not much you can do. But in general always remember that it's just stuff.

Second, start thinking about what you want to do with your stuff before it becomes a pressing matter. This is a common mistake many people make. One reason some people delay is because they just don't like thinking about death. They find it morbid. And this is a larger number than you think, as proven by the fact that two-thirds of Americans die without a will. I beg you not to make this mistake.

A second reason people delay thinking about end-of-life matters is because they sense that someone won't be happy, and they just don't want to face the negativity. Some people take the attitude that says, "I'll just let them figure it out after I'm gone." The problem is that such an approach leads to all kinds of uncertainty as the probate court steps in and starts deciding things—and probably making decisions you and your family wouldn't approve of. This does nothing to diminish the unhappiness of your heirs and adds even more sorrow and heartache at a time when they are already grieving.

A final reason people put off thinking about these matters is that it seems overwhelming, and they just don't know where to begin. The good news here is that there's a lot of help available. In Florida, for example, there is a Florida Department of Elder Affairs. There's almost no question you could have about end-of-life issues that they don't have an answer to. But there are also many other organizations and attorneys that can walk you through the process. Here are a few:

The National Institute on Aging (nia.nih.gov)

AARP (aarp.org)

CaringInfo (caringinfo.org)

National Academy of Elder Law Attorneys (naela.org)

National Elder Law Foundation (nelf.org)

I am not recommending any of these; I'm simply offering you a place to start. Any person or organization you enlist for help should be fully vetted. The point is, there's a lot of help available.

Third, consider making a positive difference in people's lives as you make your end-of-life decisions. It's good to leave your stuff to your family. But in many cases, adult children are doing fine and don't need the help. In that case, find some person or organization that *does* need the help. Your church, perhaps. Or maybe there's a special mission or organization that is close to your heart. Perhaps you were helped by an organization at some crucial moment in your life, and you would like to give back.

Fourth, remember that you can't make up for a lifetime of poor decisions by distributing your stuff in a certain way when you die. If, for example, you were a lousy father who wasn't there for your kids as they were growing up, don't think that leaving them money in your will is going to suddenly make them love you. They might be glad to have the money if things are tight, but you can be sure they won't suddenly see you as a wonderful person. Years and years of failure on your part is not suddenly going to be wiped out by an inheritance. It might even make their hard feelings harder if they believe you were trying to "buy" their goodwill from beyond the grave when you had countless opportunities to earn it when you were alive.

I want to close this chapter with a suggestion.

As you sense the end of your life drawing near—even if it's not eminent—take some time to sit down and write each of your loved ones a letter to be read after you're gone. Use this letter to thank them for the joy they brought into your life. Do a little reminiscing as you recall some experiences you shared. If there's been a problem between you in the past, make sure you grant complete forgiveness. And don't forget to offer words of encouragement. People who have received letters like this often say that they meant more than all of the material things.

In the final analysis, it's not stuff that makes life meaningful; it's relationships. When Howard Hughes died, his estate was worth $1.5 billion. He was the richest man in the world through the sixties, seventies, and eighties. But at the end of his life, he was a recluse, a drug user, and suffered from malnutrition. All that stuff couldn't bring him happiness. Your stuff won't bring

> It's not stuff that makes life meaningful; it's relationships.

you happiness either. So think about it, yes. Do the right things with it, yes. But don't depend on it for your happiness.

CHAPTER 19

STAY CONNECTED TO YOUNGER PEOPLE

It's not how old you are, it's how you are old.

—JULES RENARD, AUTHOR

John Wooden, the legendary basketball coach who won a mind-blowing ten NCAA national championships, lived to be ninety-nine. In his later years, I spent time with him to gather information for a book on his life and leadership philosophy. I'll never forget a story he told me. He said he used to go back to Martinsville, Indiana, for his class reunions, but as he got older and older, there were fewer classmates showing up. Eventually, there were only two class members left, him and a woman. When the time came for another reunion, he contacted her and said, "I'm not able to get to you, and you're not able to get to me, so why don't we just have our reunion over the phone?" She thought that was a great idea, so it was exactly what they did.

I'm not as old as Coach Wooden was then, but I am starting to experience the same dwindling of my friends and classmates. In just the last few months, I have been informed of the death of several of my high school and college teammates.

High school:

- Ruly Carpenter, pitcher (who later owned the Philadelphia Phillies)
- Gil Yule, third baseman
- Ricky Porter, pitcher
- Bill Robertson, tackle on the football team

Wake Forest:

- Don Roth, pitcher
- Bob Muller, pitcher
- Bill Covington, shortstop
- Wayne Martin, right fielder
- Bobby Brown, second baseman

Losing one friend is hard. When you lose nine in just a few months, it really makes you stop and think. Here are some things I thought about.

First, I thought about how time flies. I can close my eyes and see every one of those guys as young men. I see them on campus, in uniform, and on team bus rides. I remember their girlfriends, specific game situations, and conversations we shared. Is it possible that the things I am remembering—the things that are flashing through my mind with such clarity—happened over sixty years ago? It's more than possible; it's a fact. Very near the end of his life, Billy Graham was asked to name one important thing he had learned about life. He said, "That it passes very quickly."

If a younger person ever picks up this book and reads it, I hope by chance they land on this page and find this reminder not to take the days of youth for granted. You're young and active and have your whole life ahead of you, and then suddenly you're looking back and wondering where the years went. Nothing wakes you up to the swift passage of time like the deaths of your friends. You think, "Why are all my friends dying?" And then you realize: they're all in their eighties. Death tends to be a common problem for people in their eighties. But how did they get into their eighties so quickly?

Here's my theory.

Your mind has a way of freezing people at whatever age they were when you were involved in their lives. When you hear a name, you picture the person at that age, even if it was decades ago. Then when you meet them in person or see a current picture or hear about their passing, your mind zooms from that point in history to the present in a second or less. It feels lightning fast, even though the ticking of time has never wavered. But it is the feeling that counts, isn't it? And it feels like time flies.

Second, I thought about the durability of friendship. The word "friend" has been watered down because of social media. Facebook in particular has us using the word in crazy ways. People talk about a "friend request" as if there's nothing more to being friends than sending an electronic message and having it accepted. Or what about the "friends list" on the typical Facebook page? Is anything more ridiculous? I have a friend who has two thousand people on his friends list, but he only knows about three hundred of them, and a lot of those three hundred he has never actually met.

True friendship is about deep connections. It happens when you really get to know somebody—not the surface person but the real person. And you discover that you have things in common, that you enjoy being together, that you can trust each other. Often there is a common interest, common values, and common experience. People who have fought in a war together or played ball together or worked together often become the closest of friends.

And when a friendship is established, it is phenomenally durable. I'm sure you've had the experience of not seeing one of your friends for years, but when you finally do see them, it's as if you talked just yesterday. You pick right up with your conversation as if those intervening years never happened. It's also a beautiful thing when trouble comes into your life and you get a call from a friend you haven't seen in years but who still loves you and cares about you.

> True friendship is about deep connections. It happens when you really get to know somebody—not the surface person but the real person.

If someone asked me to make a list of the greatest blessings this world has to offer, I would have to put friendship on that list, and I would have to put it near the top. There are moments in life when nothing means more. A hand to hold, a shoulder to cry on, a listening ear, and a word of advice in a critical moment—these things are priceless, and we often get them from our friends.

Third, I thought about how important it is to stay connected to younger people. One of the harsh realities of life on the homestretch is that you can start outliving your peers. One after another, you hear about people you love dying, as has been the case with me recently. Occasionally, you'll hear about someone who has outlived all of their friends and family and are basically alone in this world. One way to keep that from happening is to make connections—friendships—with younger people.

But don't let that word "younger" trip you up.

Several years ago, when John Wooden was in his late eighties, he ran into sports author John Feinstein at the NCAA Final Four. He said, "John, what are you working on now?" Feinstein told Coach that he was working on a book about NBA coach and executive Red Auerbach, who was then around eighty. Coach Wooden said, "Oh, what a nice young man Red is!"

Younger doesn't have to mean a lot younger. It can mean just ten years or twenty years younger. I am blessed to have close friends who are in their fifties and sixties. They may not feel all that young, but to me they are. Age is such a relative thing, isn't it?

Friendships with younger people can be based on a lot of different things. I have friends that I connected with through my church and others I connected with because of our mutual love of sports. Still others I connected with as I have made my publishing journey these last fifty or so years. I am truly thankful for my younger friends, for the lunches and conversations, for the emails and phone calls, for the support and encouragement. I don't know what I would do without them.

To wrap up this chapter, let me give you some dos and don'ts for making friends on the homestretch of life.

Do broaden your horizons as you think about potential friends. That person who is young enough to be your grandson or grand-daughter might make a better friend than you think. Many highly successful people in our world were mentored by (and became very close to) people who were much older.

Do remember the golden rule of making friends: be a friend first. People who go out begging people to be their friend often end up friendless. But people who go out simply to be kind and helpful and friendly to others almost always end up with lots of friends. This time-honored principle will always be true, no matter how old you are.

Don't let your dislike of younger people's ways turn you into a curmudgeon. I know you don't like the cultural trends that young people are into. You probably hate the way they dress, the music they listen to, the tatts they get, and the way they wear their hair. But those are surface things that have little to do with the heart. If you don't prejudge them, there's a good chance they won't prejudge you.

CHAPTER 20

APPRECIATE WHERE YOU ARE

Most people are standing on a mountain of gold staring at a pile of silver in the distance.

—PATRICIA MITCHELL, AUTHOR

I've been involved with professional sports in some capacity since I got out of college, which means I've gotten to know a lot of pro athletes very well. Being a professional athlete is not as easy as it looks, especially if you're not a star. You can be cut or traded at any time if you don't produce, there's always someone younger trying to take your job, and you're always one injury away from the end of your career. This is why the average length of career in the four major professional sports is between three and five years. As many have said, "The easy part is getting to the big leagues. The hard part is staying."

That said, virtually every professional athlete is living their childhood dream. Visions of grand slam homers in the bottom of the ninth, game-winning shots at the buzzer, or touchdown passes with time running out danced in their heads as kids, and now they have a real, honest-to-goodness chance to make those dreams come true, whereas most kids with those same dreams never get the chance. Did you know that only about 2 percent of student athletes make it to the pros?

This is why I hate to hear pro athletes complain. They have been known to whine about everything from playing time to getting booed to their salary. And yes, some of their complaints are justified. But I always think about the millions of people who would happily trade places with them in a heartbeat and be perfectly happy with whatever it is they're complaining about. I know being a pro athlete is a challenging career, but it's also a gift, a rare opportunity that most people never get.

Being a senior is a little bit like being a pro athlete: not everybody gets that far, you never know how long you have left, and there's significant wear and tear on your body. If you're inclined to complain, old age will give you some fodder. One guy said, "My little black book isn't what it once was. Now it contains only names that end in MD." Another fellow observed, "I'm to the age where I no longer laugh at all those old-age remedies they sell on TV. I order them!"

> Reaching your golden years in pretty good health and with a happy, stable life is a blessing.

Yet reaching your golden years in pretty good health and with a happy, stable life is a blessing. Here are some reasons why.

First, as you age, many of the toughest challenges of life are behind you. Things like getting through school, finding a career and making something of it, choosing a spouse, raising kids, and building financial security are hard. In fact, they're so hard that some people aren't able to accomplish them. But for those who have even a moderate level of success in these areas, life can be very good.

That is not to say there won't be more difficult challenges on the homestretch. Every stage of life brings problems, and as our bodies age, there will be some for sure. But it's good to know that many hard ones are behind you.

Second, as you age, you face lesser expectations and therefore less pressure. For example, when you're thirty years old and strong as an ox, all your friends call you to help them move, especially when they have a piano that needs to be carried up to a third-floor apartment. But when you're sixty years old, you're no longer at the top of that call list.

In sports, when an aging veteran player is signed to a one-year contract at the end of his career, he is not expected to be the team's savior. Most likely, he's valued for his experience, leadership qualities, and a few on-the-field contributions here and there. Everyone knows the team is not going to rise or fall on his performance.

Even in everyday life, people who are older are not expected to carry the same load they did when they were younger. I know a doctor who now works only four days a week, an insurance man who cut his client load in half, and a college professor who no longer teaches a full schedule. They're all still engaged but with a much lighter load, and no one thinks less of them.

Third, as you age, certain benefits and privileges start to flow your way. Everyone jokes about getting their first AARP inquiry in the mail. "Oh no! I'm officially getting old!" But it doesn't take long for you to figure out that a senior's rate is a pretty nice perk. Ten or fifteen percent here and there adds up, believe me. There's also a little thing called Social Security. For years, you saw it being taken out of your paycheck and groaned. Then suddenly it starts flowing back in, and your groan turns into a smile. I've never met a senior who didn't love that day of the month when the automatic deposit lands in the bank. And don't forget about Medicare. It's not perfect, but it does help.

Fourth, as you age, your accumulated knowledge and experience help you process what happens now with less stress. It's called taking things in stride, and it's a huge factor in our happiness. A good example would be a young parent with a sick child as compared with a grandparent with a sick grandchild. The young parent feels helpless and panicky when their toddler's temperature spikes and symptoms of real sickness start to show. The grandparent, however, has seen many sick children and nursed them back to health. It's not that they take a nonchalant attitude; it's simply that they understand such sicknesses happen and that the greatest likelihood is that the child will recover and be bouncing off the walls in no time.

The same is true of cultural and economic trends.

Remember the 2020 riots that happened in cities all across America? Well, some of us remember the riots that happened in cities all across America in the 1960s.

Just recently the price of gas surged above $4 a gallon in every state. But some of us remember when the same thing happened in 2008 and when gas was rationed in the 1970s.

King Solomon said, "History merely repeats itself. It has all been done before. Nothing under the sun is truly new" (Eccles. 1:9, NLT). We feel like things are new for three reasons. One, we are young and haven't seen them before. Two, there is around-the-clock news coverage now that gives us information we didn't used to get. And three, technology puts things that happen into a different context and makes them feel different. (Like online scams, for example. Scams have always been around, but they feel different in the computer age.) The older you get, the more you understand this, and the less you overreact when something bad happens. Whatever it is, we have survived it before.

The point of this chapter is to encourage you not to fall into the habit of complaining about old age. Don't be that crusty old person who complains all the time. The homestretch of life certainly has its challenges, but it has its blessings too. Appreciate where you are. You worked hard to get here. Enjoy it!

CHAPTER 21

GIVE UP YOUR GRUDGE

There's enormous energy required to hold grudges—enormous energy! And I'm getting too old to expend my energy that way.

—ED KOCH, POLITICIAN

Thanapat Anakesri was a sixty-nine-year-old man who lived in Thailand. When he received an invitation to his fifty-year school reunion, he made up his mind to go because there was one person in particular he wanted to see. No, it wasn't an old girlfriend or his best buddy from his childhood. It was a guy who had bullied him all those long years ago.

The bully's name was Suthat Kosayamat. When Thanapat saw him, he approached him and asked if he remembered the incidents where Suthat had bullied him. Suthat did not remember, so Thanapat explained in detail what Suthat had done and asked for an apology. But Suthat said he would not apologize for something he didn't remember doing. The conversation then became heated, and witnesses say the two began to fight. During the scuffle, Thanapat pulled out a gun and shot Suthat dead.[20]

You might be thinking that a grudge nursed for fifty years must be some kind of record. Actually, it isn't. Many people have nursed grudges longer than that. They've nursed them for a lifetime. The thing that makes Thanapat's grudge so memorable is that it exploded into violence and murder.

There's no doubt in my mind that a certain percentage of the readers of this book will be nursing a grudge. Maybe you're one of them.

> No matter what was done to you—no matter how bad it was—you will have no hope of being happy on the homestretch of life if you don't let it go and forgive.

Maybe you, too, have a painful memory from decades ago that still burns like a hot coal in the pit of your stomach every time you think about it. Maybe someone bullied you, or cheated on you, or scammed you, or ran out on you. Maybe you've spent years fantasizing about how you would get back at that person if you only had the opportunity. If so, you're not alone. Research indicates that 69 percent of Americans hold grudges.[21]

No matter what was done to you—no matter how bad it was—you will have no hope of being happy on the homestretch of life if you don't let it go and forgive. There are three reasons why this is true.

---

20 Starts at 60, "Longest grudge ever? Man, 69, 'shoots former school bully dead at reunion," August 2019, February 17, 2023, https://startsat60.com/media/news/man-shoots-former-school-bull-dead-reunion-thanapat-anakesri-thailand.

21 Bryan Robinson, Ph.D., "New Study Shows The Mental And Physical Harm Of Holding Workplace Grudges," Forbes, February 2022, February 17, 2023, https://www.forbes.com/sites/bryanrobinson/2022/02/05/new-study-shows-the-mental-and-physical-harm-of-holding-workplace-grudges/?sh=77ef635b45f8.

First, grudges are 100 percent negative and offer no redeeming value at all. I've heard people talk about how a grudge fuels them and drives them to succeed. "I hate him so much I am determined to succeed and make him jealous and prove him wrong!" This may sound like motivation, but it's actually foolishness on a grand level. For one thing, with that kind of hate burning within you for years, it would be a miracle if you didn't end up with a stomach full of ulcers. Also, as you're obsessing over your mission to get back at someone, that person has likely long since forgotten about you and moved on. Imagine investing mountains of energy in such an effort, only to learn that it was all wasted because the person you were trying to get back at couldn't care less.

There's just nothing good about a grudge.

Second, a grudge will keep you focused on the past. I'll be blunt here: people who obsess over the past are almost always dismal failures. Why? Because success is about growing and building and accomplishing. And do you know what can be grown and built and accomplished in the past? Nothing! What's done is done. Whatever happened in the past is just sitting there, never to be changed in any way, no matter what you do. Even if you come up with a brilliant way to retaliate, it doesn't change what originally happened. As has been said in many an old Western movie, "You can go gun him down for killing your pa, but it won't bring your pa back."

Third, a grudge is the biggest liar of all. That grudge boiling in your gut tells you again and again that if you could just even the score, everything would be okay. If you could just teach him (or her) a lesson, you'd finally be able to release all your pent-up frustration and move on. But it's a lie, and here's why: revenge always perpetuates the conflict. *Always.* I've never seen even one case where someone who was just retaliated against said, "Okay, now everything is even, so we can stop feuding and be friends." Life doesn't work that way. When you retaliate, you're basically pouring fuel on the fire. You're literally inviting the person to come back at you hard. Far from ending the conflict, you're just setting yourself up for another round.

Fourth, a grudge negatively affects the people in your life who are not involved in the conflict. They get tired of listening to you talk about what happened. They get tired of hearing you go off every time the other person's name is mentioned. They may even worry about what you might do to try to even the score. It is not unusual for loved ones and family members to beg and plead with the grudge-holder to let it go and move on. Often a tenaciously held grudge will become a wedge between a husband and wife. Or it could go the other way. Sometimes people who love the grudge-holder will jump into the fray and get caught up in the feud themselves.

Finally, a grudge completely destroys your witness for Christ. If you're not a Christian, this may be of no concern to you. But if you *are* a Christian, it should be of utmost concern.

I'm sure you've heard the old saying, "You are the only Bible some people will ever read." The idea is that some people will never study the Scriptures to get to know God; they will only watch those of us who claim to know him and draw their conclusions from what we say and do. So if you claim to be a Christian but carry hate around in your heart, you are in essence telling the world that hate is okay, that it is compatible with Christianity. Yet even people who know nothing about the Bible know intuitively that hate is wrong, so the only choice they have is to conclude that you are a fraud, that you love your grudge more than you love Jesus.

The only answer for a grudge is forgiveness.

What is forgiveness? It's accepting what happened, giving it to God, wiping the offending person's slate clean, and going on with your life as if it never happened. I know that sounds like a bad deal for you. It sounds like the person who hurt you is getting away with it. But here's the thing you have to remember: people reap what they sow. And God is awfully good at settling accounts. In ways that you may never see or know anything about, he will deal with that person who hurt you. He promised as much when he said, "I will take revenge; I will pay them back" (Rom. 12:19, NLT).

One of your top priorities as you navigate the homestretch of life should be to jettison the baggage—*any* baggage that threatens to steal your joy and pull you toward darkness, and a grudge certainly will. No matter how justified you feel in your hard feelings, no matter how egregiously guilty the other party is, you have literally nothing good to gain from nursing a grudge. So go ahead, forgive. It's not a gift you're giving the person who hurt you; it's a gift you're giving yourself.

CHAPTER 22

MENTOR SOMEONE

A life isn't significant except for its impact on other lives.

—JACKIE ROBINSON, BASEBALL PLAYER

Long before there was a Miami Marlins Major League Baseball team, there was a Miami Marlins minor league team. It was the class A affiliate of the Philadelphia Phillies. I know because I played for them. I was a catcher out of Wake Forest, and that was where I began my quest to surpass Yogi Berra in the MLB record book.

Just kidding.

You've heard of five-tool players (throw, run, catch, hit, and hit for power)? There are people who questioned whether I was a two-tool player. I was not exactly a hot prospect. After two seasons in which I did not set the world on fire, the Phillies asked if I would be interested in moving to the front office. Yes, I can take a hint. Knowing I was not destined for big-league stardom, it seemed wise to seize any opportunity that did not involve taking foul tips off the catcher's mask—or elsewhere.

At that time Bill Durney was the general manager of the Marlins. One day I humbly asked if he could explain to me the business side of baseball. He was a very busy man, but he took me under his wing and taught me everything he knew about being a baseball executive. I was a sponge and asked a million questions. I can honestly say that everything I know about sports management, which would end up being my lifelong career, I learned from Bill Durney.

People who are on the homestretch of life may not be too spry. They may not have the energy to put in long workdays. They may no longer have the patience for a daily grind. And they may not have great health. But they *do* have knowledge and experience. There's an old Chinese proverb that says, "He knows the waters best who has waded through them." Many older people have "waded through the waters" of some worthwhile life experience. It could be anything from building a career to raising a family. And now they possess a treasure trove of wisdom.

> One of the very best ways to pass on your knowledge is to share it through a mentoring relationship.

It's sad to think about how many people die without ever passing on what they know. I've heard people say, "Yes, I have a lot of knowledge, but I could never write a book." It isn't necessary to write a book! One of the very best ways to pass on your knowledge is to share it through a mentoring relationship. Let me give you some quick tips on mentoring.

First, make yourself available. I have learned that there are a lot of younger people who would love to be mentored, but they are reluctant to ask. They think they would be imposing, that they would become a nuisance if they asked for a potential mentor's time. This is why you must make it known that you are open to the idea. If you meet some younger person who seems on the ball and shows an interest in your area of expertise, say something like this: "If I can ever help you, don't hesitate to ask. It would be my pleasure." Sometimes this is all it takes to get the ball rolling.

Second, use good judgment. There are some real no-no's when it comes to mentoring. One is mentoring a member of the opposite sex, especially if you are married. It's fine to have a conversation or two, but mentoring usually involves regular meetings, sometimes over lunch, and that kind of contact can lead to more than mentoring. Or at the very least, it can lead to the appearance of more than mentoring.

A second mentoring no-no is continuing to meet with someone who isn't teachable. Everyone seems teachable in the beginning, but often you'll see that the person isn't taking your advice, or becomes argumentative, or starts canceling your meetings. You might as well pull the plug as soon as you see it happening. Don't waste your time. Truly teachable people will be sponges.

Another mentoring no-no is trying to clone yourself. I've seen mentors get frustrated when their mentee chooses not to adopt their methods. They seem to think the person they're mentoring is somehow obligated to become their clone. No, they aren't.

The point of mentoring is to help someone reach their full potential. You share what you know, and your mentee processes it. Notice, I didn't say your mentee *duplicates* it. Duplication would be a huge mistake because everyone is different. A mentee's best course of action is to listen to what you say, process it, sift it for principles and ideas that are helpful, and then incorporate anything that might work. It might be something small or nothing at all. But the information alone is helpful because it broadens understanding.

Third, resist the temptation to try to fix someone. A person who has character flaws, who has been in trouble, who has been helped by others unsuccessfully is not a candidate for mentoring. It can be very tempting to want to try to fix someone like this, but mentoring is not a rehabilitation service. Mentoring is for people who are motivated, goal-oriented, and have high character. If you meet someone who has obvious character flaws or has recently been in trouble and yet wants to be mentored, let them prove themselves first. It is a privilege to be mentored, and people need to earn that privilege.

And fourth, be patient. Mentoring is people work, and people work is often bumpy. Consider the term "late bloomer." It was coined to describe people who matured and developed slower than most other people. Sometimes in mentoring you can get a late bloomer, a person who may have the raw talent to be successful but for whatever reason just doesn't put it all together quickly. If you see that the character and desire is there, be patient. The point is not to bring someone to maturity quickly but to do it eventually. Remember the tortoise and the hare.

Arturo Sandoval is arguably the world's greatest trumpet player. He's won ten Grammys and been nominated nineteen times. You could say he is the Michael Jordan of trumpet players. As a young Cuban musician, he met American jazz legend Dizzy Gillespie. Dizzy took Arturo under his wing and mentored him. Eventually, Sandoval defected to the United States and built a career that has touched virtually every musical medium, from live performances to recordings to film scores. If you ever hear Arturo interviewed, you will hear him talk at length about Dizzy's influence on his life. And if you look at any of the YouTube videos that he makes in his home, you will see pictures of Dizzy on practically every wall.

What is the value of having someone love and respect you that much?

It's another reminder that selflessness will enrich your life. When you come to the end of your days, not many things will seem all that important. But one thing that *will* seem important is the piece of yourself you left behind in some person who is now better and more able to enrich others because of your influence.

CHAPTER 23

SURPRISE PEOPLE

If wrinkles must be written upon our brows,
let them not be written upon the heart.

—JAMES A. GARFIELD, FORMER PRESIDENT OF THE UNITED STATES

As this chapter is being written, Mike Freemont is one hundred years old. He holds five world records, which is five more than all but a small handful of people in the whole world. If that's not amazing enough, consider that he didn't start setting these records until he was eighty. And if *that's* not amazing enough, consider that all of his world records are for running.

Yes, running.

He set the record for the fastest marathon time at age eighty and then again at age ninety. He holds the fastest half-marathon record for ages ninety and ninety-one. And he holds the record for the fastest mile at age ninety-six. A cynic might say, "But at that age he couldn't have had much competition." True. But even if he didn't have *any* competition, it's incredible that he could run these races at such an advanced age.

But even *that's* not all there is to Mike Fremont's story.

In 1992 Mike was diagnosed with colorectal cancer and told that he had three months to live. Doctors removed the cancerous tumor and found that it had not spread. Mike soon recovered from the surgery and decided that one of the best ways for him to thumb his nose at the cancer that brought such a scare into his life was to start running competitively. In his last competitive marathon, Mike set a world record for ninety-year-olds at six hours and thirty-five minutes.

As I've already mentioned in this book, there's a lot of stereotyping of older people. The thing I like most about Mike Fremont is that he absolutely destroyed every old-people stereotype there is. This is a noble goal for anyone who's on the homestretch of life. Don't let yourself be pressed into the little box the world has created for you. Surprise them!

Here are some ways you can do this.

First, stay active. Recently, I read about a softball league in Boston. It is called "the Golden Years Senior League" and boasts ninety players on seven teams. Most of the players are in their seventies and eighties. One gentleman who plays in the league said it's not uncommon for play to be stopped so the players can gather around and look for somebody's hearing aid that fell out. Talk about teamwork!

> Don't let yourself be pressed into the little box the world has created for you. Surprise them!

Obviously, not everyone on the homestretch of life is going to be able to play softball. But there might be other things you can do. One eighty-plus-year-old lady in Kissimmee, Florida, got a job at a doctor's office as a "waiting room hostess." She greeted everyone who walked through the door, kept things straightened up, and served coffee to patients who were waiting.

Just down the street from there was an Italian restaurant. Whether the owner got the idea from the doctor, I don't know, but the restaurant had a "dining room hostess." Again, it was a woman in her seventies who carried a basket of breadsticks, doling them out like candy to customers along with smiles and friendly greetings.

All of these people could have been at home, piled up in a recliner, watching television. That's what we would expect. But they defied the stereotype and surprised people.

Second, stay interesting. Talking about your latest doctor appointment, or how long it took you to get there, or how that medication he prescribed affects your bowels is not interesting. People will nod and act interested because they are polite. But they will probably be zoning out, especially if you told them all about it the last time you talked.

Imagine how pleasantly surprised someone would be if, instead of reciting the details of your medication side effects, you started talking about a thought-provoking book or article you had read. Or even better, imagine how surprised someone would be if you didn't talk about yourself at all but simply asked questions.

"Seen any good movies lately?"

"Where's your favorite place to go on vacation?"

"Do you have a favorite restaurant?"

"Tell me how you met your wife (husband)."

Do you realize that people will think of you as being interesting if you just ask questions? You don't even need to say much. If you just ask questions and listen and nod while people talk, they will walk away thinking about how pleasant it is to talk to you. And they will be surprised.

Third, stay open-minded. One of the biggest raps against older people is that they are prejudiced against anything new—anything that's not from their generation—whether it's fashion, music, technology, movies, you name it. Trust me when I tell you that younger people find nothing so tedious as listening to an older person complaining about the younger generation. Imagine if *you* had to sit and listen to younger people complain about *your* generation. You wouldn't like it either!

The secret to staying open-minded is to remember that every generation of older people hates the fads and trends of the younger generation, yet somehow Western civilization manages to survive, and those younger people grow and develop into halfway decent adults. Isn't that amazing? So the next time you're tempted to go on a long rant about everything that's wrong with "these kids today," don't. Try talking about something new—a product or technology—that has been a help to you. I promise, you will surprise people.

Fourth, stay real. Someone who isn't authentic is a pain at any age. But older people have a reputation for not being willing to admit they're old. Do you remember the commercials that showed an older woman lying on the floor, saying, "Help! I've fallen, and I can't get up!" This is a very real horror for older people. Falls happen all the time, and many of them result in life-threatening injuries or even death. So a device was invented that would enable a fallen person to press a button and summon help. There was just one problem: nobody wanted one.

Sales of such devices were far less than expected because so many people refused to admit that they might need one. And here's an even more astonishing fact. According to German researchers, 83 percent of people who owned such a device and fell on the floor refused to press the button.[22] They preferred to suffer and struggle and try to get

---

22   Adam Gopnik, "Can We Live Longer But Stay Younger?," The New Yorker, May 2019, February 17, 2023, https://www.newyorker.com/magazine/2019/05/20/can-we-live-longer-but-stay-younger.

up by themselves than to call for help because calling for help would be the same as saying, "I am old."

If you want to surprise someone, don't try to convince them that what they know isn't true. Don't act like things that are difficult for you are a piece of cake. When your friends and neighbors try to help you, don't act offended and lecture them about how you're not over the hill just yet.

One surefire way to stay real is to joke about your age. I heard about an older woman who was telling her best friend about the new exercise class she was taking. She said, "I bent, twisted, gyrated, jumped up and down, and sweated for an hour. But by the time I got my leotards on, the class was over."

Don't be a typical old sourpuss who reinforces every negative stereotype about old people. Be fun. Surprise people!

CHAPTER 24

WEAR COMFORTABLE CLOTHES

Stay true to yourself. An original is worth more than a copy.

—SUZY KASSEM, POET AND PHILOSOPHER

I have a reputation for wearing Hawaiian shirts. Let me explain how it happened.

I arrived in Florida in the summer of 1986 to work on bringing an NBA franchise to Orlando. Naturally, I had important people to meet and meetings to attend, and in the interest of not making them wonder why in the world such a clod was hired, I wore a suit and tie. Looking and acting professional is on the first page of the Leadership 101 handbook.

The problem was, it was a million degrees outside with 100 percent humidity—or at least it felt like it. I had never been so uncomfortable in my life. What's more, I saw the men I was working with looking perfectly miserable as well. And then I asked myself a simple question: why? The tie is probably one of the dumbest ideas in the history of man anyway, but when you wear one in extreme heat, it becomes more than dumb; it becomes insane. So I decided that if I was going to live in Florida, I was going to be comfortable. I started wearing Hawaiian shirts everywhere I went.

And then a strange thing happened.

People got such a kick out of my decision to buck the system that they started congratulating me and even buying me shirts! "Here, Pat, I saw this and knew you'd like it, so I got it for you." Suddenly, I was accumulating Hawaiian shirts right and left. And I wore them. Often I was the only guy at a function who didn't have a coat and tie on. The funny thing is, other guys would look at my shirts longingly, dreaming about how nice it would be to dress like me and be comfortable. But they didn't have the courage to break out of the mold.

I'm sure it won't surprise you to learn that this chapter isn't really about shirts or how you dress. It's really about thinking for yourself and doing what works for you, regardless of what other people might think. If you're on the homestretch of life, I'm guessing you spent most of your life jumping through hoops and trying to meet other people's expectations. Now, my friend, it's time to do things *your* way. Here are some thoughts worth considering.

First, many of the traditions and expectations that are placed on us are just plain dumb. Wearing a coat and tie in extreme heat is one, but there are others. Not long ago I heard Elon Musk talk about how he runs his companies (Tesla and SpaceX). He said he tells his employees that if they are attending a meeting that isn't helping them, he expects them to get up and walk out and go back to work. It's better to be productive than to sit in a pointless meeting wasting time.

> Many of the traditions and expectations that are placed on us are just plain dumb.

I wanted to stand up and cheer!

Do you realize that every single business day, millions of people all around the world sit in tedious, boring, pointless meetings secretly contemplating ways to put themselves out of their misery? Most companies have too many meetings. Way too many. But the employees, like sheep, are expected to flock into the conference room and listen to all the pointless pontificating.

Another ridiculous practice is spending $30,000 for a wedding. That's right, $30,000 is the average cost of a wedding in America today. That's the cost of a nice new car or a down payment on a house, things that might actually help a newlywed couple. I can remember when a wedding was a preacher, a punch bowl, and a cake. Now couples spend $1,500 on the invitations alone and send them to people they don't even like because they feel obligated. Like the guy who runs all those boring meetings at work!

You know it's true. Many of the expectations that are placed on us are just plain dumb. God bless you if you can find the courage to say "Nope. I'm not doing that."

Second, it's important to remember that civilization will not collapse if you decide to think for yourself. I have many friends who are preachers, and it's fun to sit and listen to their stories about how their church members cling to tradition. One told me about the time he decided to move the Communion table to the back of the auditorium instead of leaving it in front of the pulpit where it had been for many years. The idea was that, by having the ushers serve Communion from the back of the room, it would be less distracting for worshippers who were trying to pray and have an intimate moment with God.

As you can probably guess, there was an uprising the likes of which hasn't been seen since Custer's last stand. One lady said that if the table wasn't returned to its "proper" place, she would have no choice but to find another church. After all, one can only tolerate so much foolishness from a young whippersnapper of a preacher. Wisely, the preacher left the table in the back. The lady stayed (after considerable huffing and puffing), and the church prospered with no Communion table in front of the pulpit. Imagine that.

This is what happens most of the time when you make an outside-the-box choice. A few narrow-minded people puff up and bluster, and then things settle down, and life goes on.

Third, you might actually be doing others a favor by going against ingrained expectations. Right now it is common for men to wear sneakers with a suit and tie. You see this everywhere but especially on television sports pregame shows. I'll admit that the first time I noticed this, I thought, "What's wrong with those guys? Didn't anyone ever teach them how to dress?" But then a funny thing happened. The style became more and more widely accepted and started to seem normal!

But think about this: somewhere, someone was the first guy to make the move from dress shoes to sneakers. I don't know who he was. I'm sure he got razzed about it. But now men everywhere are praising his name or would be if they knew who he was. Without realizing it, the man was liberating all the millions of men in this world who hate dress shoes.

Back when I made my switch from suit and tie to Hawaiian shirt, I caused a bit of a stir. Some said, "I wish I could get away with doing that." I needed a pithy quip to respond with but didn't have one. Then one day I heard Larry Dierker, the former all-star pitcher, say something that I adopted as truth and decided to borrow. He pointed out that in all of recorded history, there's no record of anyone ever having a bad day while wearing a Hawaiian shirt.

What might be your Hawaiian shirt? Is there something you've always done that you've never liked or enjoyed simply because other people expected you to do it? Is there a way you could lighten your load, reduce your stress, or make your life more comfortable by stepping away from traditional expectations? If so, and if it won't hurt anybody, I challenge you to do it. You've earned the right, and it will make you much happier on the homestretch.

CHAPTER 25

DOUBLE-CHECK YOUR VALUES

Nowadays people know the price of everything
and the value of nothing.

—OSCAR WILDE, AUTHOR

I heard a story about a man who was driving down a road in his pickup and saw a sign out in front of a farmhouse. The sign said, "Talking dog for sale. $10." The man thought that was probably some kind of joke, but curiosity got the best of him, and he decided to stop and check it out.

When the farmer answered the door, he said, "Yes, I really do have a talking dog, and if you want him, you can have him for ten bucks. I'll be glad to get rid of him." The man was still skeptical, so he asked to see the dog. The farmer said, "Follow me," and led him out the back door to an old doghouse. The dog poked his head out, and the farmer said, "Duke, this man would like to meet you. Why don't you tell him a little about yourself?"

The dog said, "Be glad to. I started talking at an early age. The CIA found out about it and trained me to do undercover work. They sent me on dangerous missions all around the world. I was responsible for catching several international terrorists and have even received several medals for valor in the line of duty."

The man was dumbfounded. He looked at the farmer and said, "This is the most unbelievable dog I've ever seen. Why in the world are you selling him for $10?"

The farmer said, "Because all he does is lie. He never worked for the CIA a day in his life."

Unfortunately, a lot of people are like that farmer: they undervalue things that are priceless. This is particularly easy to do through our young adult and middle-age years. When we are young, we often undervalue things such as virginity (90 percent of people have sex before marriage), our faith (66 percent of people stop attending church when they go to college), and our health (recklessness and substance abuse are the leading causes of injury and death in young adults).

Then when we get older and enter middle age, we start undervaluing other things, such as marriage (the divorce rate among couples in their fifties is at an all-time high) and financial health (people age forty-five to fifty-four have the highest rate of credit card debt in the country).

All of this leads to a moment that many people experience. Maybe you have. It's that moment when someone looks in a mirror and wonders how he got so far away from what he was taught when he was young. I am always amazed at the number of people who were raised well by God-fearing parents but who drifted into a completely different kind of life as they grew older. A life that is not as good, not as happy.

We can debate how this happens, but clearly one cause is that our values change. The wrong things start becoming important to us.

For that reason, I recommend that you spend some time reflecting on your current values. How have they changed? Are they making your life better or worse? Was there a time in your life when your values were different and you were happier? Do you sometimes feel empty and frustrated with your life and wonder what went wrong? These are hard questions but good questions. As you reflect on them, consider these truths about values.

> No matter what happens, your reaction should always have love in it.

First, some values are eternal and should never change. The importance of love is a good example. No matter what happens, your reaction should always have love in it. That's not to say you can't be angry or frustrated if someone mistreats you. But even when that happens, there is always a response that has love in it. Perhaps instead of firing back at that person, you hold your tongue or refrain from getting revenge. You might still be ticked off, but the love in your response would keep things from escalating and relieve you of the burden of having to keep score.

On the subject of loving responses, I can tell you from personal experience that always striving for a loving response to every situation will make you happier. A friend of mine once pointed out to me that First Corinthians 16:14 says, "Do everything in love," and challenged me to commit myself to fulfilling that command, to see how long I could go without getting angry or frustrated with someone. I happened to be leaving on a speaking trip, so I said, "Okay, on this trip, no matter what happens, I will give a loving response every time." Naturally, the hotel staff messed up my reservation, and I had a big problem when I arrived, so I was tested right out of the gate. But I was Mr. Loving Response. I swallowed my frustration and was as nice and considerate as I could possibly be. When I got home, Ruth asked me how my trip went, and I told her that I honestly thought it was the most enjoyable trip I'd ever been on. And it was! Not because everything went smoothly but because my mindset was one of love.

Another eternal value is generosity. The world is full of wonderfully generous people. I am amazed at the outpouring of aid every time there's a natural disaster anywhere in the world. It is truly heartwarming. But it's equally true that many people become less generous as they get older, as their debt and their standard of living increase. They figure they need every penny just to pay the bills, many of which they chose unwisely to take on. Often you will hear someone say, "I would love to give, but I just can't right now. Money's too tight." And they're telling the truth. What they're not saying is that it's their own fault.

Think about eternal values such as love, generosity, kindness, work, service, and others. Are there some that you used to prioritize but don't any longer? If so, ask yourself why. What do you need to do to get back to them?

Second, some values should change with the seasons of our lives. Things that were once important to me aren't any longer. Competition is an example. As you might guess, I am a highly competitive person. I used to obsess over ways to make the team I was leading the best one in the league. Every draft pick, every free agent signing, every coaching hire caused me sleepless nights. I was determined not to fail. But eventually I entered into a different season of life, and now those things don't concern me at all. I'm thrilled to let someone else handle that responsibility.

Parenting is another example of a value that changes. When our kids are young, they are our life. Virtually every waking hour is spent thinking about them and providing for them. But they eventually grow up—both they and you enter into a different season of life—and the constant concern and obligation subsides. Not the love, of course, just the constant responsibility. No longer do you consider your kids first when you make a big decision, and it's okay. They don't even live with you anymore.

Third, some values carry more weight than others. For example, people-related priorities are going to have a much greater impact on my life than object-related priorities. In Orlando there was a guy who took great care of his car. By "great" I mean he washed it almost daily. Whenever he came home from driving it—even if it was just to the grocery store—he would retrieve a soft cloth from his garage and wipe it down from stem to stern, not missing an inch. The car was probably five years old, but it sparkled like it did the day it rolled off the new car lot. But then the man and his wife got a divorce, and he moved out.

Think about that.

It's a fine thing to take care of your car. Cars cost a lot of money, and a wise person will prioritize keeping it in great shape. But taking care of your car is not as important as taking care of your marriage. I don't know what went wrong in their marriage, but I can't help wondering how things might have turned out if he had been as attentive to his wife as he was to his car.

You get the point. All values are not created equal. I encourage you to spend time thinking about the heavier, weightier values in your life. The ones that are people-related.

The good thing about values is that they can be adjusted at any time. If you realize that you have drifted away from values you once held dear, you can fix the problem with a decision. You can choose to help your wife carry the groceries into the house instead of running to grab your cloth so you can wipe down the car.

CHAPTER 26

DEVELOP A SMART RETIREMENT STRATEGY

Often when you think you're at the end of something,
you're at the beginning of something else.

—FRED ROGERS, TV'S MR. ROGERS

Let's talk about retirement. There are several common attitudes toward it.

The first attitude toward retirement is to want to retire as soon as possible. This attitude is common among people who don't like their jobs. They long to escape like a fish longs for water. I've known people who weren't scheduled to retire for years, but they could still tell you exactly how many days they had left until retirement. Now you can even set your watch to count down the days, hours, minutes, and seconds. I suspect that app was created by a guy who hated his job.

A second attitude toward retirement is to never retire. I've heard preachers say, "I want to drop dead in the pulpit in the middle of a sermon." (Personally, I hope I am sick that day. I think I would be traumatized.) And then of course, there's the old adage, "I'd rather burn out than rust out." I get the sentiment, but I'm not sure it's as noble as it sounds. Most of the burnout cases I have known have been miserable people with awful, broken relationships. There's a reason why people who are burned out often need counseling and a long vacation.

And the third attitude toward retirement is the one I endorse: step away from your main job so that you don't have to punch a clock and do the daily grind anymore but stay busy with worthwhile projects and activities that make a difference in people's lives. Some people call it semiretirement. I like to call it "tapping the brakes." You slow down a little, but you're still moving, still going places, still making a difference.

I bring all of this up because there is a simple way to be happier on the homestretch of life, and that is to develop a smart retirement strategy. Here are some suggestions that will help you.

First, live within your means. People talk about how they're going to do this and that when they retire. "I'm going to travel" is a common refrain. One guy vowed that he was going to travel to every Major League ballpark to see a game. That's great! But don't forget, traveling costs money. If you've got it, go! But if you don't, be careful. According to Bloomberg, only about 3 percent of retirees have enough money to do everything they want to do.[23] The last thing you want to do is ruin your retirement by overextending yourself financially.

Second, stay disciplined. When you're working every day, you have a schedule to keep: a time to get up, to leave the house, to arrive at work, to leave work, to arrive home, to go to bed, and so on. The

---

23   Suzanne Woolley, "A Comfortable Retirement Appears Out of Reach for
       Most Americans," Bloomberg, May 2022, February 17, 2023, https://www.
       bloomberg.com/news/articles/2022-05-24/most-americans-say-1-1-million-
       they-need-to-retire-comfortably-is-out-of-reach?leadSource=uverify%20
       wall.

routine may seem dull, but it gives your life structure, and structure can actually help you hold things together. If you abandon all structure when you retire, it may feel good at first. In fact, it may feel great. But without some structure, you can start drifting aimlessly and feeling a little lost. Many people who couldn't wait to retire will tell you that they don't like it as much as they thought they would, and this is usually the reason. They need to be disciplined and have some structure, even if it isn't as rigid as what they had when they were working.

Third, eat healthy and exercise. Many people who are working full time will say that when they retire, they're going to start eating better and exercising. "I'm always on the run now, and I don't have time, but when I retire, I'm going to prioritize my health." This is another one of those things that's easier to say than do. If you've reached the

> It's never too late to improve your health.

age of retirement without developing good health habits, it's going to be hard to start from scratch. I'm not trying to discourage you; I'm just being real. It's going to take some hard work, but I encourage you to do it. It's never too late to improve your health.

Fourth, exercise your mind. The one fear that most of us share as we grow older is losing our mental sharpness. One way you can help yourself stay sharp is by exercising your mind. I've already told you I am a big proponent of reading. I read two to three books per week, and I can assure you that it makes a difference. At eighty-two, I have certainly lost a step in the one-hundred-yard dash (or maybe twenty steps, or thirty, or more), but my mind is as sharp as ever. Ideas still flow through my head a mile a minute. I'm still doing three radio shows a week and writing books. I don't believe that would be the case if I didn't keep my mind as active as I do. I encourage you to read,

read, and read some more. Read whatever interests you. The world is full of wonderful books on every conceivable subject. You could also work puzzles and play games that challenge the mind, like chess, for example.

Fifth, seek out new social contacts. When you're working every day, you have coworkers and associates, some of whom you will enjoy and interact with beyond the workplace. Then suddenly you don't see them anymore. Along with your job go the water cooler conversations, the lunches at the corner deli, the football watch parties with the guys, the Christmas parties, and so on. Sometimes when retired people feel a sense of discontent, it's nothing more than the fact that their social life has been disrupted. Their friends are suddenly missing from their daily routine, and they feel the void. One way to combat this feeling is to make new friends. Take up a new hobby, join a club, do volunteer work. Even one new friend can bring some freshness into your life.

Sixth, spend time outside. Unless you had a job that required you to work outside, you probably spent most of your working years cooped up inside an office or warehouse. For that reason, you may not realize what a mood lifter the outdoors can be. In fact, more than just lifting your mood, outdoor activities can actually improve your mental health. The technical name for it is "ecotherapy," and it has proven very effective in helping people who suffer from anxiety and depression. At the very least, you will benefit from going for a walk every day.

The great thing about your retirement is that it's *your* retirement. You can do with it whatever you want. That thought alone is exciting, isn't it? Doesn't it give you all kinds of ideas of things you'd like to do? I say, do them! But be smart. Use good judgment. You'll get much more out of your retirement if you do.

CHAPTER 27

LEARN TO RECEIVE

If we counted our blessings instead of our money, we would all be rich.

—LINDA POINDEXTER, WRITER AND HUMORIST

A touching story comes from Kim Campbell, country singer Glen Campbell's wife, who was married to him for thirty years and walked by his side during his final years as he suffered from Alzheimer's. In 2012 Glen did a farewell tour. By that time Alzheimer's had taken a heavy toll on his mind. He was able to perform, but sometimes he would forget lyrics or even what he was doing. Occasionally, he would wander off stage in the middle of a number, completely confused. Yet he wanted to do the tour. He loved his fans and wanted to say goodbye. His band and crew were up for the challenge and showed tremendous patience.

One night on that tour, the group stayed in a bed-and-breakfast in Michigan. Glen got up early and went downstairs with a member of the crew. In the gift shop, he saw a sign that had the words "Mother's Day" on it. He said, "Mother's Day! I want to buy Kim a Mother's

Day present! She loves pink. I want to get her something pink!" So he started looking and found a bottle of Pepto-Bismol. He took it to the register and was about to purchase it when Kim came down the stairs and saw what was happening. She hurried over and gently took the bottle from Glen's hands, saying, "We don't need that, Glen," and returned it to the shelf. She thought it was an impulsive, for-no-reason purchase that had become common as his Alzheimer's worsened.

It wasn't until later that the crew member who had accompanied Glen downstairs was able to tell Kim that Glen had seen the Mother's Day sign and was determined to buy her a gift and that it had to be something pink because he knew she loved that color. In her memoir Kim said, "My jaw dropped. I had no idea. Tears filled my eyes. A wave of loving gratitude washed over me ... My dismissive action robbed him of a chance to express his love. It also robbed me of receiving that love."[24]

Those are important words. Read them again.

"My dismissive action robbed him of a chance to express his love. It also robbed me of receiving that love."

I have noticed that people on the homestretch of life can be very dismissive of those who are trying to give to them.

"I don't need any help. I can do it myself."

"I can pay for my own meal. I'm not destitute, you know."

"I don't need a ride. I'm perfectly capable of driving myself."

"Don't get me anything for Christmas. Spend your money on the kids."

I suppose the reason older people say these things is that they're desperate to cling to whatever degree of independence and self-sufficiency they have left. They think that if they start letting people do

---

24 Kim Campbell, *Gentle on My Mind* (Nashville: Thomas Nelson, 2020), 224.

things for them, that means they really are old. It's the same reason older people are reluctant to start using a cane or a walker. It's not so much the help but what the help says about them.

But Kim Campbell was right. When you resist or block the impulse of people to give to you, you are robbing them of the joy of expressing love. And you are robbing yourself of the joy of receiving it. Here are some thoughts to consider.

> When you resist or block the impulse of people to give to you, you are robbing them of the joy of expressing love. And you are robbing yourself of the joy of receiving it.

First, stubbornly refusing the help of others doesn't make you seem younger; it only makes you seem stubborn. Here we are back to the idea of older people often being cranky or curmudgeonly. The subject keeps coming up because it's so often true. And this is one of the reasons: we find anything—even a gesture of kindness—that makes us feel old and needy offensive.

But here's a news flash: people who want to help you—who offer to do things for you—aren't doing it because they think you're old and needy. They're doing it because they love you. Has it occurred to you that when someone offers to give you a ride, it's not because they think you're incapable of driving but simply because they'd like to spend time with you? And if someone picks up your check at lunch, it's not because they think you're broke but because you've been a blessing to them and they want to show some appreciation?

As older people, we really need to stop reading something negative into the situation when someone tries to do something nice for us. Don't look for insinuations or hidden messages. Sometimes people really are just trying to be nice.

Second, when you graciously let people do things for you, they are receiving a much greater gift than you are. Jesus said, "It is more blessed to give than to receive" (Acts 20:35, KJV). Have we forgotten this?

There's an old story about a nobleman who was traveling to a nearby city with his servant. At one point, they came upon a beggar, a pitiful man beside the road who was wearing rags and looked emaciated. The nobleman stopped and dug some gold coins out of his pocket, tossed them to the beggar, and wished him well. As they rode away, the nobleman's servant said, "Sir, why did you give that man gold coins? Someone that poor would have been happy with copper coins." To which the nobleman replied, "I didn't give him gold coins to make *him* happy. I gave him gold coins to make *me* happy."

Major League Baseball gives the Roberto Clemente Award each year to the player who best exemplifies outstanding character, community involvement, and contribution to his team. That second factor—community involvement—is huge. The winners typically receive the award because of enormous contributions of time and money to help people in need all around the world. What's interesting is that almost all of the winners say that winning the Clemente Award means more to them than the baseball awards they have won. And we're talking about MVP and Cy Young Award winners. There's a simple reason why they get a bigger blessing from giving than from playing: it's more blessed to give than receive.

Third, the best way to respond to giving is not by resisting the gift but by becoming a giver yourself. I love the concept of "paying it forward." If you're going through a drive-through and the person at the window informs you that the car ahead of you paid for your order, don't chase that driver down and explain to him that you have money of your own and don't need his help. Simply put a smile on your face, thank

God for the blessing, and then pay for the order of the car behind you. Think of how the kindness and joy would be multiplied!

At my age I understand as well as anybody the temptation to do things for myself and not depend on others. My first reaction is always "I can handle it. I don't need any help." But sometimes the point isn't that you need help. The point is that someone is trying to be nice to you. Don't rob them of the blessing they will get from that. And don't rob yourself of the joy of receiving their love.

CHAPTER 28

TRY ... OR TRY AGAIN

The only failure is not trying.

—ROBIN S. SHARMA, AUTHOR

I love hearing about people who accomplish big things later in life.

Frank McCourt, for example, won the Pulitzer Prize for his book *Angela's Ashes*. What's crazy is that he didn't decide to try to write until he was sixty-five years old.

At the age of sixty-two, Harlan Sanders franchised his secret fried chicken recipe and gave the world what we now know as Kentucky Fried Chicken.

James Parkinson was sixty-two when he identified Parkinson's disease.

Rosa Branicka was sixty-three when she developed new surgical techniques for breast cancer by operating on her own tumor. (The surgery was successful, and she lived to be eighty-two.)

Actually, this list could go on forever. We often think that history's great accomplishments are achieved by middle-aged people and younger, but that is not true. Many of them are achieved by older people, and many who are on the homestretch of life.

As I write this book, I am eighty-two and working on bringing Major League Baseball to Orlando. I have a reputation for being a basketball guy, and I am. But more than anything, I am a baseball guy. It was my first sporting love when I was a boy and still holds a special place in my heart. Demographics show that Orlando is ready for a Major League Baseball team, so I began figuring out what it would take to get one, either through expansion or relocation. It's my answer when anyone asks if there's one more important thing I'd like to accomplish before I go to be with the Lord. If we are successful, I will consider it the greatest accomplishment of my life.

What about you?

Is there something you've never tried to do but always wanted to? Is there something you've become interested in as you've grown older that you think you might like to try? Is there something you tried to do years ago that didn't work out and now feel like trying again? Well, what's stopping you? One of the great things about the homestretch of life is that we often have more time than we had when we were younger. I often hear people talk about the "empty nest" when their kids leave home. To me, a nest should never be empty. When your kids leave home and there's suddenly more room and time, you should fill it. Do something new, or go back and try again to do something that didn't work out the first time.

> One of the great things about the homestretch of life is that we often have more time than we had when we were younger.

Speaking of trying again, my retirement years have been devoted to trying to bring Major League Baseball to Orlando for the third time. Yes, the third time. We gave it a shot in 1990–91 and then again in 1995. Both times we struck out. When I retired from the Magic and thought about what I wanted to do in my retirement, I decided the third time might be the charm. Maybe there's an unreached goal from your past that you should try again.

There are a couple of reasons why the things we try to do when we're younger don't work out. One is that the timing isn't right. People are sometimes too busy with jobs and kids to give their full devotion to a project. They might *want* to give their full attention, but other responsibilities keep pulling them away. Second is a lack of money. Many projects require an investment. I can't count the number of times I've heard people say, "We had to give it up because we ran out of money." It's encouraging to know that after a lifetime of working and saving, we often have both more time and more money when we retire.

Here are two things I often hear people who are on the homestretch of life talk about wanting to do.

The first thing I hear people on the homestretch of life talk about wanting to do is write a book. Sometimes it seems to me that everybody wants to write a book. I hear people say it all the time. Often I ask, "What would your book be about?" The answers are all over the map, but one of the most common ones is "My life." I have good news and bad news about that answer.

The bad news is that unless you have done something truly mindblowing, no publisher is going to want a book about your life. I know you think your life story is interesting, and it probably is … to you and your family and friends. Unfortunately, a publisher wants your story to be interesting to millions of people. You know why they need millions to be interested? Because only a tiny percentage of people who know your name and find you interesting will fork over $25 for a book. They might like you and admire you and think you're cool.

And they might check your book out of a library or buy it in a thrift store for a dollar. But they're not paying full price for it. So if you haven't cured cancer or invented flying automobiles, there's very little chance you're going to get a book deal about your life from a big New York publisher.

That's the bad news.

The good news is that in today's world, you don't need a traditional publisher to write a book. You can write your life story and, for a reasonable amount of money, have it published yourself. And here's why you should: your current family and future descendants will love it and cherish it.

I was twenty-two when my father died at the age of fifty-five. I hadn't yet reached the age where we ever sat down and talked about his life as a young man. Later, when I was in my thirties and forties, I began wondering more about his life and experiences. I would have loved to quiz him about it, but it was too late. Oh, how I wish he had written down his stories. Further, my father's grandfather (and my great-grandfather), Charles Williams, fought in the Civil War for the confederacy and was captured. I can't imagine the stories he had, but he never wrote them down.

You have seen things and done things your loved ones would love to know about too. Sure, you've probably told a lot of stories over the years, but it's the ones they haven't heard that would mean so much to them. What a gift it would make to your loved ones!

Don't worry about not being a professional wordsmith. The company you work with will have an editor. The main thing is to get your story down and share it with the people who love you.

The second thing I hear people on the homestretch of life talk about wanting to do is lead someone to Christ. I understand this because it's become a passion of mine as I have gotten older. In an earlier chapter,

I mentioned that several of my high school and college friends and teammates have died in the last couple of years. I am happy to say that I witnessed to all of them. The results weren't always what I wanted, but I tried. I found that I couldn't *not* try. The older I get, the more I realize that it's important to be ready to stand before God. I want to be ready, and I want others to be ready.

Is there someone you need to witness to? Or maybe someone you need to witness to again? If so, do it! Here are a couple of thoughts that I hope will motivate you.

One is that evangelism is, by nature, a process more than an event. Yes, we have stories in the Bible about people making instantaneous decisions to follow Jesus, but those are the exception rather than the rule. Most people need to ponder and pray and process what they hear. I've known people who have taken years to finally make a decision for Christ. That can be very frustrating to those of us who want to see them saved right now, but it's better than them not accepting Christ at all.

Another encouraging thought is that people's circumstances change and can make them more open to Jesus. This is especially true of older people. When people are young and healthy, they are often too obsessed with their careers to think about spiritual things. But some creaky bones and scary diagnosis from the doctor can make them more willing to listen. Perhaps you can think of someone you have witnessed to before who is in a completely different life situation now, one that would make them more receptive.

The point of this chapter is to encourage you to stay busy. Think of what it is you want to try, or try again, and do it. Add your name to the long list of people in history who made their homestretch years count.

CHAPTER 29

WORK ON YOUR LEGACY

*If you would not be forgotten, as soon as you are dead and rotten,
either write things worth reading, or do things worth writing.*

—BENJAMIN FRANKLIN, FOUNDING FATHER OF THE UNITED STATES

As we age we tend to think deeper thoughts than we do when we're younger. For example, at some point along our life journey, we start thinking about what we're going to leave behind—our legacy. Not many twenty- and thirty-year-olds are doing that. But when we reach our fifties and sixties, yes. And it's good that we do think about it because we all leave a legacy. Whether you've been intentional about it or not, you've been building one and will continue to until you die. So what's it looking like?

What will people remember about you when you're gone?

How many people will smile when they think of you?

How many people will talk about how you helped or inspired them?

How many people will remember your example or some lesson you taught them?

One of my greatest influences was Mr. R. E. Littlejohn, who owned the Spartanburg Phillies when I became their general manager at the age of twenty-four. I've written about him extensively in many of my books. His influence on my life was so profound that even to this day, I often ask myself, "What would Mr. Littlejohn do?" Your influence doesn't have to be *that* profound to be significant. The main thing is to leave behind a legacy that is positive and helpful. Here are four ways you can do that.

First, be honest at all times. We are living in a world where people don't even expect to be told the truth. In politics, for example, our elected officials and press secretaries step up to the mic, look right into the camera, and say things they know are not true. Fact-checkers practically hyperventilate as they point out falsehood after falsehood, but it doesn't stop the lying. A recent survey indicated that 75 percent of people tell one or two lies a day, and that lies comprise 7 percent of all communication.[25]

> Your influence doesn't have to be *that* profound to be significant. The main thing is to leave behind a legacy that is positive and helpful.

The world is starving for honesty and truth. If you are scrupulously honest and truthful in all your dealings, you will stand out the way a unicorn would in a corral full of ponies. And people will appreciate it and respect you for it. And remember when you're gone.

Second, be careful what you say. It's possible to be truthful in everything you say and still do damage with your tongue. Every husband who's ever been asked, "Does this dress make me look fat?" knows

---

25   Tony Docan-Morgan, "How often do people lie?," Currents, November 2021, February 17, 2023, https://www.uwlax.edu/currents/how-often-do-people-lie/.

this very well. So while we are being truthful, we also need to think about the impact of our words, how they feel when they are heard. When hard things need to be said, we should look for ways to soften the impact so that the truth doesn't get lost in an emotional response. This does *not* mean we should water down the truth to the point that it has no impact; it simply means we should be like Mary Poppins and use a spoonful of sugar to make the medicine go down.

Also, with regard to our speech, we should avoid all profanity and vulgar talk. I know, I know, you can't watch TV for five minutes without hearing profanity. And many movies have hundreds of curse words. Even bookstores now feature books that have the vilest curse words, not just in the content but in the titles! (When I'm in a bookstore and see one of these books, I make it a practice to turn it over so that the cover can't be seen.) Profanity and vulgar talk may be common, but it is never good. It always taints the user. Yes, some will laugh at a dirty joke and others may take cursing in stride, but if you want to set a good example for young people and show respect for those who don't want to hear junk speech, you will watch your mouth.

Third, be an encourager. I was at an event where Truett Cathy was speaking to a group of young people. I was to speak after he finished, so I stood in the wings and listened. I remember him saying this: "You know who needs encouragement? Everyone who is still breathing." He was right.

The late Florence Griffith Joyner, better known as Flo-Jo, was a track-and-field athlete who won both gold and silver medals in the 1988 Olympics. She told me that one of her greatest sources of inspiration was the legendary boxer Sugar Ray Robinson. When she was only eight years old, she met him. Like any celebrity, he was busy and in a hurry, but he paused long enough to speak with her and encourage her dreams. She said, "Right then and there, I was sold. I was just eight years old, but I was all fired up about what my future could be."

You are always around people who need encouragement. You know how I know that? Because *everybody* needs encouragement! Not just eight-year-old kids who dream of being track stars but also people of all ages in all walks of life. This is a difficult world we live in. We all have bad days. We all face challenges. If you consistently offer people encouragement when others are scolding or criticizing them, you will be loved and appreciated. And someday people will be talking about you the way Flo-Jo talked about Sugar Ray Robinson.

Fourth, be generous with your time and resources. A friend of mine ate lunch at a certain Mexican restaurant every Thursday. He always sat at the same table and was always served by the same young woman. There was a language barrier because the server spoke very little English, but with some pointing and pantomiming hand signals, they were able to communicate. Since my friend always ordered the same thing, it eventually got to the place where he just walked in and sat down, and the server brought him his food.

After a full year of this, Christmas came. My friend wanted to show the young woman his appreciation for so many days of excellent service, so he left her an unusually large tip and wished her a merry Christmas. When she saw the cash, she broke into tears and in seconds was sobbing. My friend was stunned and asked her what was wrong. In very broken English, she said that she was a single mom with several kids, and she did not have enough money to buy them Christmas presents. But with this extra amount of money, she would be able to go shopping after work and get them some gifts. Then they were both crying.

My friend was never going to miss the money he gave her. I won't say it was nothing, but really, to him it almost was. But to her it was everything. Generosity is one of the greatest attributes a person can possess and one of the most impactful.

The late Bobby Bowden was one of the greatest college football coaches who ever lived and a good friend. He won 377 games in a sport where only 13 were played each season. Let that soak in. He also won two national titles and numerous conference championships. Many people wondered why he kept coaching until he was eighty. He had won all the trophies and awards and had nothing left to prove. His answer was interesting. He said that he loved influencing young men, and he couldn't do that from his easy chair.

Bobby was everything I just encouraged you to be.

He was honest, careful with his words, full of encouragement, and generous with his time and resources. His players, all of whom revere him, do so not because he won football games but because of the kind of man he was. People will revere you also, not because you're good at your job but because you're good to them. It's never too late to start building a good legacy.

CHAPTER 30

GET RIGHT WITH GOD

We turn to God for help when our foundations are shaking,
only to learn that it is God who is shaking them.

—C. WEST CHURCHMAN, PHILOSOPHER

I am a man of faith. I gave my life to Jesus Christ many years ago and have done my best to live for him ever since. I believe in heaven and look forward to going there someday. In fact, my faith in salvation through Jesus Christ is what makes a lot of the difficult stuff I have faced in this world bearable. A few years ago, when I was diagnosed with multiple myeloma, I was determined to beat it. But it sure was nice to know that if I didn't, I had a mansion prepared for me in heaven. It was like I couldn't lose: If I lived, great! But if I didn't, I knew I would be in a better place.

I can't think of a single thing that's more important for people on the homestretch of life to think about than their relationship with God. With death creeping ever closer, it's important to know that you're saved. Allow me to share some important thoughts on the subject as I wrap up this book.

First, your salvation is between you and God. When I witness to people, I often begin by asking, "Do you believe there is life after death?" Recently, I asked an unsaved friend this question. She answered, "No, I think this is it." I shared with her my belief that there is more, that there is heaven and hell, and we will all spend eternity in one or the other. But there was nothing I could do beyond that. Her decision about the matter is between her and God.

And yours is between you and God.

Other people (like your spouse or parents or a friend) might take an interest in your decision. If you have a pastor, he most certainly will. But when all is said and done, it's not their call; it's yours.

A few years ago, I received news that a man I knew quite well had died. He was well into his nineties but was in good overall health and had a sharp mind. Perhaps we should never be surprised when someone in his nineties dies suddenly, but in his case, I was. That's how healthy he seemed.

I found out later that the man enjoyed online betting on sporting events. His son, who knew of his dad's love for online gambling, thought he ought to check his dad's computer. It's a good thing he did. He discovered that on the afternoon of his father's death—perhaps minutes before his father died—he had placed a bet on a major sporting event and won about $600. His son collected the winnings and took the money to his father's clergyman. "Here," he said, "take these winnings for the church. I want to make sure my dad gets into heaven. This should take care of it."

The son meant well, of course. He cared about his dad. But his actions demonstrate several misunderstandings. First, the Bible makes it clear that you can't buy your way into heaven. Salvation is repeatedly said to be "free" (Rom. 6:23). Second, once you're dead, there will be no more chances to be saved. Your friends won't be able to come along after the fact and do for you what you chose not to do for yourself during your lifetime (Heb. 9:27). And third, one person can't "pull strings" to make sure another person gets into heaven. Salvation is a personal matter between you and God (Rom. 10:13).

Second, there's a lot of confusion about how salvation happens. Probably the majority of people in the world believe that salvation is all about what you *don't* do. Ask the average person why he believes he's going to heaven, and he'll likely say something like this: "I'm a good person. I don't lie, cheat, steal, or curse. And I don't judge people."

Other people believe they are going to heaven because of what they *do*: "I go to church every Sunday and serve on two committees and pay my tithe every week. I also give extra to help with special projects and missions."

And still other people believe being saved is all about pedigree: "My granddaddy was a preacher, and my daddy served on the church board for twenty years, and my momma has taught Sunday school for as long as I remember. Of course, I'm a Christian!"

I've always felt that confusion and misinformation are two of Satan's most effective tools. We picture him with a pitchfork and tail, stirring up terrible trouble. And he *does* do that. But I am convinced that merely confusing people and making them believe things about God and salvation that aren't true are his bread and butter. Never forget that in the Garden of Eden, he didn't attack Eve and try to kill her; he simply told her a lie (Gen. 3:4–5).

Third, we don't need to be confused about how to get right with God because the Bible makes it very clear. It all starts with faith. The Bible says that without it, you simply can't please God, no matter what else you do (Heb. 11:6). But what is faith, you ask? Simply put, it's believing what you can't see. You can't see God or Jesus. You weren't around when Jesus was performing miracles. You didn't see him being nailed to the cross or witness his resurrection. But if you've studied the evidence for these things and have come to the conclusion that they are true, you have faith.

Second, the Bible teaches that getting right with God involves inviting Jesus to come into your heart as Savior and Lord and then obeying him. Both parts are important. The second part (obedience) proves that the first part (making Jesus your Lord) is real. Some people seem to think they can just say some magic words and then go on doing whatever they want, but the Bible says that "faith by itself, if it does not have works, is dead" (James 2:17, NKJV). Simply put, you can't just talk the talk; you have to walk the walk.

> The Bible teaches that getting right with God involves inviting Jesus to come into your heart as Savior and Lord and then obeying him.

You might ask, "But, Pat, what if I mess up? I started out obeying God, but I got offtrack for a few years and didn't live for him. What do I need to do?" That's an important question because just about everybody gets into that situation sooner or later. We're all weak and, like sheep, prone to wander away. But never fear; the Bible tells us exactly what to do when our obedience flounders: repent.

The word "repent" means "turn around and go in the opposite direction." So if you mess up and let your relationship with God fall into a sorry state, you simply need to stop doing whatever bad things have gotten you into trouble and start doing the right things. In other words, correct whatever has gone wrong. It may not be easy if you've allowed yourself to settle into some bad habits, but you *can* do it if you really want to.

Is that what you need to do today?

If so, I encourage you not to wait.

Dwight L. Moody (1837–1899) was the founder of the Moody Bible Institute. On November 16, 1899, he preached what would be his final sermon in Kansas City. People who came out to hear him that day were shocked at how he acted and looked. In just a few short weeks, he had put on a lot of weight and looked bloated and unhealthy. Little did they know that he was suffering from congestive heart failure, a condition that would be quickly and easily diagnosed and treated today but not then. Moody, however, sensed that he was dying and that the time was coming soon. He said to his friends, "Soon you will read in the newspaper that I am dead. Don't believe it for a moment, for I will be more alive than ever before."

That kind of assurance is only possible when you know you have gotten right with God. In this book I've talked about a lot of things you can do to be happy on the homestretch, but nothing is more important than this. Whatever life throws at you as you age, whatever physical, mental, and emotional challenges you have to deal with, you will still be able to smile if you know all is well between you and your Heavenly Father and that you have eternity in heaven with him to look forward to.

A FINAL MESSAGE FROM PAT

Several years ago I attended a San Diego Padres baseball game with my friend and well-known pastor David Jeremiah, who was in his sixties at the time. At one point during the game, I said, "David, do you ever think about retiring?" Immediately, he flared up. Adamantly, he said, "Why would I retire? Everything I do feeds off of my preaching—the TV, the radio, the books ... all of it." Then he said, "Pat, you never want to be a *former* anything." Sure enough, David is now in his eighties and still going strong.

Of course, David would be the first to acknowledge that sometimes retirement is forced upon us. But even then we have a choice to either fade into oblivion or to keep going, keep producing, keep accomplishing. May this book be a friendly reminder to you never to quit living your best life so that your later years truly can be your greater years.

ABOUT THE AUTHOR

Pat Williams, longtime NBA executive and basketball Hall of Famer, is currently leading an effort to bring Major League Baseball to Orlando. He is the author of well over a hundred books, many of them on leadership. Pat is the father of nineteen children and has twenty-one grandchildren. He lives in Orlando and can be reached at pwilliams@patwilliams.com.

ABOUT THE WRITER

Mark Atteberry is the award-winning author of nineteen books. He was a pastor for forty-six years before retiring in 2020. He now writes full time, producing both fiction and nonfiction and assisting other great thinkers who have messages he believes in. He lives in Kissimmee, Florida, with his wife, Marilyn. Mark can be reached at markatteberry93@gmail.com.

9 781642 258790